Better Parties, Better Government

Better Parties, Better Government

A Realistic Program for Campaign Finance Reform

Peter J. Wallison and
Joel M. Gora

The AEI Press

Publisher for the American Enterprise Institute
WASHINGTON, D.C.

Distributed to the Trade by National Book Network, 15200 NBN Way, Blue Ridge Summit, PA 17214. To order call toll free 1-800-462-6420 or 1-717-794-3800. For all other inquiries please contact the AEI Press, 1150 Seventeenth Street, N.W., Washington, D.C. 20036 or call 1-800-862-5801.

Library of Congress Cataloging-in-Publication Data

Wallison, Peter J.
    Better parties, better government : a realistic program for campaign finance reform / Peter J. Wallison and Joel M. Gora.
        p. cm.

Includes bibliographical references and index
    ISBN-13: 978-0-8447-4270-0 (hardcover)
    ISBN-10: 0-8447-4270-8 (hardcover)
    ISBN-13: 978-0-8447-4271-7 (pbk.)
    ISBN-10: 0-8447-4271-6 (pbk.)

    1. Campaign funds—United States. 2. Political parties—United States.
3. Elections—United States. I. Gora, Joel M. II. Title.

    JK1991.W34 2009
    324.7'80973—dc22

                                                                 2009007698

13 12 11 10 09   1 2 3 4 5

Printed in the United States of America

Contents

List of Illustrations

Acknowledgments

Peter Wallison would like to thank Joel Gora for reminding him what good lawyering is like, and Karen Dubas of AEI for her invaluable research work and assistance in putting together the book.

Joel Gora would like to thank his co-author and friend, Peter Wallison, for suggesting the collaboration that produced this book; Jane Dryer, for her excellent research assistance; and the Brooklyn Law School Dean's Summer Research Stipend Program for supporting his work on this project.

Introduction and Summary

The campaign finance system in the United States is unusual in one major respect: it is candidate-centered. The candidates themselves, rather than the political parties, must raise the necessary funds to run a campaign. The political parties, which choose the candidates—or at least run the process under which their candidates are selected—are severely restricted in their ability to finance their candidates' campaigns.

As a system purportedly designed to reduce corruption and undue influence—and upheld against First Amendment challenges on this basis—a candidate-centered fundraising system seems, to say the least, rather odd. Among other things, it places the candidates and officeholders who need campaign funds in exactly the position they should not be occupying—as supplicants, seeking financial support from those who are trying to influence them.

As one might expect, there was a reason for structuring the campaign finance system in this peculiar and contradictory way: as we show in chapter 1, it is highly favorable to the incumbents who designed it. But it also has a number of other deficiencies: it favors wealthy candidates who can finance their own campaigns; it piles up campaign funds in the coffers of powerful officeholders where these funds are not needed; it discourages qualified people from running for office; it absorbs an extraordinary amount of the time and attention of officeholders, who should be spending most of their energy on the responsibilities of their offices; it increases the costs of campaigns by increasing the role of expensive consultants and other campaign specialists; it deprives voters of useful information; and it multiplies the power of special interests at the expense of a broader national interest. Most of all, it weakens the political parties, which alone have the ability both to develop popular support for a course of action and implement it with legislation.

All these deficiencies, and more, will be explored in this book, and none has been addressed in all the campaign "reform" efforts that have characterized the last four decades. In fact, most of this legislation has made things worse, particularly for challengers; only the Supreme Court's invalidation of the most egregious pro-incumbent elements of the so-called reforms has preserved for challengers some limited opportunities. Still, the remaining restrictions—on the size of contributions and, most important, on the ability of parties to fund the campaigns of their candidates—continue as substantial obstacles for those who seek to defeat incumbent members of the House and Senate.

The current restrictions on campaign funding by political parties limit both the amount that parties can contribute to their candidates and the amount that parties can spend in coordination with their candidates. In the leading case in this area, *Buckley v. Valeo*, the Supreme Court held that campaign-related spending coordinated with a candidate is the same as a contribution, and thus could validly be restricted by Congress.[1] In two subsequent cases, the Court held—on First Amendment grounds—that political parties had the same rights as others to engage in unlimited "independent" or *uncoordinated* spending on behalf of their candidates,[2] but that they could be restricted in their coordinated spending because party contributions could become a route by which party contributors could influence officeholders.[3]

Thus, as the law stands today, parties are severely limited in what they do to provide direct assistance to their candidates, but are as free as any other group to spend funds independently—on an uncoordinated basis—in support of the candidates running for office under the party banner. However, independent or uncoordinated spending is generally considered by candidates and political specialists to be far less efficient and effective than coordinated spending, and is often counterproductive.[4] As Thomas Mann of the Brookings Institution has pointed out, "diminished efficiency and accountability" are the costs of requiring that parties' spending be independent of their candidates: "Having to set up a separate independent spending operation increases the administrative expenses borne by parties. More importantly, it runs the risk of conflicting messages and less than optimal timing of ads run by candidates and their parties."[5]

Consider some of the specific restrictions dictated by current law. Party committees are allowed to give directly only $5,000 per election to their

House candidates and $39,900 to Senate candidates. The $5,000 cap on contributions to a House candidate is the same amount that it was in 1940, and would be worth about $65,000 in today's dollars; the cap for a Senate candidate would be $519,000. While parties can make coordinated expenditures of $42,100 in support of their congressional candidates (the coordinated expenditure limit with Senate candidates depends on the number of voters in the state and is commensurately larger), the continued persistence of caps and coordinated expenditure limits seriously hinders the important role of political parties in our political system and is an uncomfortable reminder of the incumbent-protective nature of contribution limits.

These limits significantly impaired the ability of both major political parties to provide direct or coordinated support to their candidates in the Senate and House races in 2008. In that year, for example, all Senate races cost a total of $389 million. Of this amount, direct party contributions totaled $694,000 (0.18 percent), and party coordinated expenditures were $5.4 million (1.4 percent). The story was pretty much the same in House races. There, all campaigns cost $808 million, party contributions were $1.8 million (0.22 percent), and party coordinated expenditures were $8.1 million (1 percent).[6] These sums were dwarfed by the amounts that the parties spent on an uncoordinated basis in support of their candidates. In all Senate races, for example, party committees spent $117.7 million on an uncoordinated basis (30.2 percent of the total cost), and in House races, uncoordinated expenditures by party committees were $109.5 million (13.6 percent).[7] To be sure, coordinated and uncoordinated party funds are not distributed evenly among the campaigns. In 2006, for example, most of these funds were in the form of uncoordinated spending in support of a relatively few campaigns where the parties thought they had a good chance to win. Of the amount spent to support Senate and House candidates, 61 percent (approximately $151 million) was concentrated on five Senate races in Missouri, Ohio, Virginia, New Jersey, and Tennessee, and on fifteen House races. In those races, party spending ranged between $4 million and $6 million.[8]

The public is generally unaware of the distinction between direct and independent expenditures by parties, because the media does not make the distinction in reporting party financial support for candidates. From the standpoint of candidates and political professionals, however, the differences between the two types of financing are significant. In 2007, Senators Corker and Bennett introduced S 1091, a bill to eliminate restrictions on parties' financing of their candidates. In the only hearing that was held on the bill, Senator Stevens noted that "oftentimes the candidate himself or herself does not quite agree with the party in some of the advertising they bring into the state,"[9] and much of the discussion in the hearing was about how to address the problem of an uncoordinated party ad hurting a candidate's campaign, and whether a candidate would be able to get such an ad taken down without violating the Federal Election Commission (FEC) rules on coordination.

As might be expected if the purpose of restrictions on party financing is to undermine the campaigns of challengers, the line between coordinated and uncoordinated spending is diligently policed by the FEC, an agency composed of three Democrats and three Republicans that is carefully watched by Congress for any deviations from a strict interpretation of the campaign finance laws. In the most recent campaign reform legislation, the Bipartisan Campaign Reform Act of 2002 (BCRA), also known as McCain-Feingold after its two principal Senate sponsors, Congress vacated then-existing FEC rules that defined coordinated expenditures and directed the agency to develop a more broadly based definition.[10] The broader the definition of coordinated spending, of course, the tighter the restrictions on communications between parties and candidates. As campaign finance expert Trevor Potter has noted, the FEC finds evidence of coordination in "inside knowledge of a candidate's strategy, plans, or needs; consultation with a candidate or his or her agents about the expenditure; distribution of candidate-prepared material; or use of vendors also used by a candidate."[11]

If not carefully structured, uncoordinated expenditures could bring an FEC fine, or worse. Violation of campaign finance laws—even technical violations—are widely reported in the media and of course harmful to candidacies. Without an agreement between the candidate and the party as to the scope of the party's independent expenditures—an agreement that might destroy the "independent" character of the expenditure—the candidate must engage in extensive fundraising anyway. Under these circumstances, only direct contributions to a candidate's campaign, or expenditures coordinated with the candidate, are truly useful to candidates, but these are restricted by the campaign finance laws.

Although uncoordinated party spending is by far the largest portion of the permissible spending by parties, it is only a small portion—generally less than one-fifth—of the total cost of running a campaign for the Senate or the House of Representatives. For this reason, parties are important but limited campaign finance sources for their candidates; ultimately, candidates know that they are largely on their own. There is no reason why this should be true; as we will argue in this book, parties are inherently better and more efficient fundraising vehicles than the candidates themselves. If freed from the current restrictions, parties could—and, we believe, would—become the primary source of campaign funds for their candidates.

This will cause, in our view, two major and salutary changes in our political system. For the first time in many decades, incumbents will face serious opposition from well-funded challengers, and campaigns will quickly become more competitive. We discuss this issue in chapter 3. The second change, discussed in chapter 4, involves a new and unaccustomed role for the parties. Today, the parties are largely service and support organizations for candidates, but with the ability to finance their candidates' campaigns, the parties are likely to gain a more important voice in the policymaking process. We believe this will substantially improve our politics and our government system.

Political parties play important roles in every democracy, but their functions are determined by the constitutional arrangements that exist in each country. In parliamentary systems, the head of the governing party is often the prime minister. If the party achieves a parliamentary majority, its policies and program are implemented by the government. If a coalition is necessary to achieve a majority, the dominant party is forced to compromise its policies and program in order to form a government with the participation of minority parties that have different views.

The current structure of political parties in the United States—as service organizations rather than policymaking bodies—has led to elections that have little programmatic content, and congressional majorities that do not have specific mandates. The result is that policymaking defaults to the presidency, largely because presidential candidates are forced to state their views on current issues in the course of a presidential campaign, and these views become a kind of platform for the party that holds the White House. The congressional majority that is elected at the same time—whether or not of the president's party—generally has no identifiable mandate. That is why presidents have only a short period—a "honeymoon"—during which they are able to implement the program on which they sought election. After that, the power of special interests fragments a Congress that has no lodestar or set of goals.

The one exception to the general rule that Congress has no specific mandate is the Republican-majority Congress elected in 1994 after Newt Gingrich "nationalized" the election with his "Contract with America" campaign. That election, and its immediate aftermath, showed that a party could propose and implement a specific set of reforms if it had the ability to offer its candidates the necessary financing and gain their consent to support the party's program. We discuss this possibility in chapter 4.

Deficiencies of the Candidate-Centered Campaign Finance System

Before we make our case for a party-centered campaign finance system, it is necessary to detail how the current candidate-centered system harms our politics.

Enhancing the advantages of incumbents. In our electoral system, incumbency offers substantial advantages. In elections in which there is no overriding issue of national importance, almost all incumbents who choose to run are reelected. Barring sweeping voter revolts, such as the elections of 1994 and 2006, changes in House and Senate membership generally occur because of deaths, retirements, or decisions to run for higher office. This is not healthy for a democracy, and one of the goals of campaign finance reform should be to reduce or minimize the inherent advantages of incumbency and thus make our elections more competitive. Parties and the candidates competing for votes will be more responsive to the voters, before and after the election. This seems obvious, so the fact that our current finance system adds to the advantages of incumbents is clearly a deficiency.

The advantages of incumbency arise from many factors; among the most significant are the perquisites of office, which provide incumbents with a government-paid staff to carry out constituent service and allow incumbents to stay in contact with their constituents at government expense; the ability to make local news at will; and the opportunity to bring federal money into a district or state through the appropriations process. These are inherent

advantages and cannot be significantly reduced without impeding representatives' ability to communicate with voters or properly carry out their duties.

Incumbency also provides financial advantages, first of all because a
lawmaker sits on committees that have considerable regulatory power over
large sectors of the economy. No matter what the lawmaker's policy positions,
there are bound to be many political action committees—specialized political
financing vehicles known as PACs—and individuals who will either benefit
by, or fear harm from, the lawmaker's votes on issues of importance.
Campaign contributions could be a way to increase a lawmaker's support for
proposed legislation, and in any event provide a basis for gaining access to the
lawmaker or his staff. The fact that incumbents are likely to be reelected
increases the incentives of PACs and individuals to provide financial support.
In this way, incumbents, even junior members of Congress, are able to build
campaign fund war chests for their reelection campaigns. In addition, the
name recognition that goes along with incumbency makes fundraising easier,
and the opportunity to build a war chest during the time in office usually
means that incumbents are better prepared with funds and staff at the outset
of a campaign than are challengers.

A challenger, unless independently wealthy, faces a very different financial environment. PACs and individuals, afraid to incur an incumbent's
disapproval, are often unwilling to contribute even to challengers with whom
they agree. (In this sense, disclosure of contributions—commonly praised
by both supporters and opponents of the current system—also creates advantages for incumbents.) Contributions to challengers generally come in slowly,
so that it takes a long time for a challenger to accumulate enough funds to
engage a complete campaign staff.

Given the inherent advantages of incumbency listed above, it seems reasonable to suppose that challengers have to spend more than incumbents in
order to have a chance of winning. Yet, with few exceptions, incumbents generally are able to raise and spend more than challengers. In 2008 Senate races
where the incumbent won with more than 60 percent of the vote—in other
words, where the incumbent was a virtually sure winner from the outset—
the mean level of the incumbent's expenditures was $5 million, while the
mean level of the challenger's expenditures was $1.2 million. In more com-
petitive Senate races that year, where the incumbent won with less than 60
percent of the vote, the incumbent's mean expenditure was $10.9 million and

the challenger's $4.3 million. In 2008 races where incumbent senators were defeated, they still outspent their opponents $10.2 million to $7 million.[12] In 2008 House races, the mean level of expenditures on reelection by incumbent representatives was $1.1 million where the incumbent won by more than 60 percent of the vote; in these races, the challenger's mean level of expenditures was $227,546. In more competitive races, where the incumbent won with less than 60 percent of the vote, the mean level of incumbent expenditures was $2 million, while the challenger's was $1.1 million. In House races where incumbents were defeated, they still outspent their challengers $2.3 million to $1.9 million.[13]

There are very few options available to reduce or mitigate the advantages of incumbents in fundraising. Restricting spending, one idea that is frequently advanced for this purpose, would likely have a contrary result. While restrictions on spending would leave both the incumbent and the challenger with similar financial resources, the incumbent's inherent advantages in name recognition and constituent communications and service would place him far ahead of most challengers. In any event, the Supreme Court has invalidated restrictions on spending as violations of the First Amendment's guarantee of free speech, unless a candidate voluntarily agrees to the limits. Accordingly, within the four corners of current campaign finance laws, there is no obvious way to rectify the imbalance in favor of incumbents or to put challengers in a financial position to overcome the inherent advantages of incumbents. The only way this can be done is to introduce a new source of financing for challengers—a source that has a built-in incentive to provide funds for challengers. This source is the political party, which has one central purpose—to gain or retain political power through electoral success. Thus, the most efficient way to create a level playing field—with challengers able to compete effectively with incumbents—is to eliminate the restrictions on political parties that currently prevent them from financing the campaigns of their own candidates.

It is clear that incumbents have recognized this. By limiting the role of parties in providing funds for their candidates, Congress—in other words, incumbents—made sure that challengers would seldom have the same campaign finance resources as those who have already attained office, and almost certainly never more. It is hard to discern another plausible reason for the restrictions that current campaign finance laws place on political parties.

It could well be true, as some might argue, that a candidate-centered fundrais-ing regime conforms to the localized nature of elections in the United States. But the fact that candidates might not *need* or even want party financing is not a reason to restrict it by law.

That officeholders have set up a financing system that favors incumbents should remind us why mandatory government financing of political cam-paigns will not work. (Chapter 2 evaluates this and other proposed reforms to the current system.) In such a government-financed system, there is no alternative to the rules Congress establishes for the financing of campaigns. The government will be the exclusive source of the funds needed by incum-bents and their challengers. As they have shown in all recent campaign reform efforts, however, members of Congress will manipulate the law and the regulations in order to make it difficult for challengers to get traction. As unwieldy as a private system of campaign finance may be, it will, if properly structured, at least make it possible for private individuals and groups to oppose the incumbent group; an unfettered ability to "throw the bums out" must be seen as the most basic right available to the voters in a democracy, and this right can be guaranteed only by a private campaign financing system, insulated as much as possible from the depredations of Congress.

Creating the appearance of corruption or buying influence. If the original Federal Election Campaign Act (FECA), adopted first in 1971 and amended substantially in the wake of Watergate in 1974, was truly intended to pre-vent either corruption or the appearance of corruption, it was very poorly designed.[14] By focusing the fundraising process on the candidates them-selves, FECA and the most recent reform law, the Bipartisan Campaign Reform Act, both have the effect of forcing candidates into the compromising position of seeking financial support from the very people who want some-thing from *them*.

The obvious deficiencies of this system have stimulated reform after reform since 1971, but in no case was a change in the candidate-centered fundraising system seriously considered as an alternative. The interplay between what Congress finally adopted and the Supreme Court's rulings under the First Amendment has distorted the reform legislation in a number of ways, but has left its basic structure largely intact. As a result, the media never cease to point out that candidate X is receiving campaign funds from special interest Y, implying that this accounts for candidate X's position on issue Z. The equally plausible alternative—that Y is contributing to X's campaign because Y agrees with X's position on issue Z—is seldom if ever mentioned. We should not be surprised under these circumstances that voters are cynical about elected officials and even the campaigns themselves.

If we are serious about reducing corruption or the appearance of corruption, there are only two choices—a government-financed system, or one in which private campaign finance continues but candidates are able to find financing without directly soliciting funds from those seeking influence. We have suggested above how incumbents could manipulate a government-financed system to their advantage; such a system would permit Congress to create the worst possible perversion of democracy—a regime in which it is nearly impossible to dislodge incumbents.

However, if political parties become the principal fundraising vehicles for political campaigns, the possibility of corruption or the appearance of corruption will be significantly attenuated. Not only will the substantial fundraising of parties dwarf any particular contribution from a person or group, but the party's interest in developing and enacting a broad-based political program will also mean that the special interests of various contributors will be submerged in a broad coalition the party will have to assemble.

Favoring wealthy candidates. Frequently, we read in the press that a political party is looking for a candidate who can finance his own campaign. The parties seek such candidates because our current campaign finance law, as interpreted by the Supreme Court, places no limits on what an individual can spend to get himself elected. Compare this to what another individual or a PAC can contribute to the same campaign ($2,300 and $5,000 respectively). If a wealthy person can be identified who will finance his own campaign, the party does not have to compete for funds with its own candidate, and the campaign is likely to be better run and financed from the outset than a campaign by someone who has to start from scratch to raise the necessary funds.

The existence of this seemingly anomalous situation—in which an individual can contribute as much as he wants to his own campaign but not to the campaign of anyone else—says a great deal about both the intentions of Congress when it enacts campaign finance legislation and the views of the Supreme Court concerning the scope of this legislation. Congress's initial effort at campaign finance reform was the Federal Election Campaign Act of 1971, which imposed a cap on what any candidate (along with the candidate's immediate family) could spend on his campaign—$50,000 for presidential candidates, $35,000 for Senate candidates, and $25,000 for House candidates. This cap remained in place when the Federal Election Campaign Act Amendments of 1974 were adopted, and other restrictions on contributions and spending were imposed.

The 1974 amendments were then tested in the courts, and *Buckley v. Valeo*, the leading case, reached the Supreme Court in 1976.[15] In its *Buckley* decision, the Court concluded that campaign contributions and spending were essential elements of the First Amendment's guarantee of free speech, and accepted only one legitimate basis for restricting campaign contributions or expenditures: the possibility or appearance of corruption. Following out this logic, the Court then struck down all expenditure limitations—it could find no appreciable link between these limits and corruption or the appearance of corruption—as well as limits on contributions by a candidate to his own campaign. After all, the Court reasoned, how could a candidate corrupt himself? But the Court upheld strict limits on contributions *to* candidates.

Buckley, then, left incumbents exposed to challengers who had the personal wealth that enabled them to finance credible campaigns—a problem (from the perspective of incumbents) that Congress attempted to rectify in the BCRA. In that legislation, Congress adopted what is known as the "Millionaire Amendment," which raises the contribution limits for a House candidate facing a challenger who contributes more than $350,000 to his own campaign.[16] This amendment, of course, is yet another example of the incumbent-benefit focus of campaign finance "reform." Although its language is even-handed—that is, both incumbents and challengers are partially relieved of the contribution limits if they face a candidate who contributes more than $350,000 to his or her campaign—in reality incumbents never have to contribute significant amounts to their own campaigns after they gain office, so no challenger would ever have been able to make use of the Millionaire Amendment.

In 2008, the Supreme Court also struck down the Millionaire Amendment, finding that it was not based on preventing corruption or the appearance of corruption.[17] The Court's opinion, written by Justice Alito, contained an extensive discussion of the inherent advantages of incumbents and noted that the Millionaire Amendment could not "be justified on the ground that it served 'the ancillary interest in equalizing the relative financial resources of candidates for public office.'"[18] Thus, not only did the Court in this case reassert that the only basis for restrictions on contributions and expenditures was corruption or the appearance of corruption, but it also specifically discounted the notion that campaign finance reform could, under the First Amendment, have the purpose of equalizing the financial resources of challengers and incumbents.

The political system in the United States should be better than this; participation in elective office should be possible for all qualified people, regardless of the costs of gaining office. Allowing parties to finance their candidates' campaigns will make substantial amounts of campaign funds immediately available to the best candidate—not the wealthiest—that the party or the party's voters in a primary election can find.

Discouraging high-quality people. The difficulties associated with raising funds to challenge an incumbent, or even to run for an open seat, are likely to discourage many people who might otherwise make themselves available as candidates. Highly qualified people, who would make fine lawmakers, will not consider running for office because they cannot finance their own campaigns and quail at the thought of spending hours on the telephone begging for financial support. In addition, many highly qualified people recognize that even if they win office they will be required—notwithstanding the advantages of incumbency—to begin the fundraising process all over again if they want to be assured of reelection. In the case of House members, fundraising for the next election begins immediately after they've won the most recent contest.

As a result, when they search for candidates, parties are not able to select from among the best potential candidates in a state or district; they must pick from among those who are not offended and demeaned by the need to raise their own funds. Poor candidate quality, then, should not be surprising. In the lead-up to every election, we read reports of parties and party leaders trying desperately to recruit high-quality candidates to run for seats that are regarded as contestable. More often than not, they seem to fail and have to settle for candidates who are second or third best, and frequently for someone whose principal qualification is that he can afford to finance his own campaign.

Another familiar press story is about the prominent and successful law-maker who could easily win reelection, but abruptly announces his retire-ment. Often, he identifies the endless and painful process of fundraising as the reason for leaving office. If the process of fundraising were good training for public office, or if it involved skills that would enhance our representa-tives' effectiveness in office, perhaps it would make sense to subject candi-dates to this test. But successful fundraising doesn't tell us much about the quality of the candidate as a legislator; instead it raises suspicions about his honesty or objectivity on issues of public importance. Running for and hold-ing a public office is a trying experience, and we should bend every effort to make public office accessible to the most qualified people the parties can find. Permitting parties to finance their candidates' campaigns would bring higher-quality candidates into the field.

Distracting elected officials from performing their functions. Even law-makers who have the intellectual and other resources to perform well in office may be distracted from their important roles by the fundraising neces-sary to remain there. In an election year, which occurs every other year for members of the House of Representatives, a representative may have to spend half his time trying to corral the funds necessary to improve his chances for reelection, especially in light of the unrealistically low contribu-tion limits. Fundraising, along with returning to the district for four-day weekends, seriously depletes the time available for attending committee hearings, for learning about the issues coming up for a vote, and for doing the many other chores involved in enacting legislation. Accordingly, apart from exposing candidates and elected officials to an appearance of corruption, the current system also makes it difficult for them to do the jobs they are actually elected to do.

What's going on here? When we elect people to serve as our representa-tives and senators we should expect them to devote all their working time to their duties. The current system does not offer that prospect. With the excep-tion of the few committee chairs and wealthy or favored candidates, members of Congress must devote huge amounts of time to fundraising rather than doing the work they were elected to do. While it might be argued that a certain amount of fundraising puts the representative or senator in closer touch with his constituency, the returns from this effort rapidly diminish. In the complex world of today, we should want our elected officials to spend their time learning about issues, not "dialing for dollars." Giving the parties a larger role in campaign finance would allow elected officials to perform their duties.

Promoting inefficient or wasteful use of campaign contributions. The distribution of campaign contributions is yet another area where the current system fails. Campaign contributions are very unevenly distributed. Some committee chairs and other powerful incumbents receive more campaign funds than they need. They then use these funds for their own purposes, such as assisting colleagues, and often provide their surplus funds to their party's congressional or senatorial campaign committees. There are no limits on the amount of these contributions, which again demonstrates the financing advantages of incumbency. In 2006, members of Congress gave $83.2 million to party campaign committees. Most of this money came from their personal war chests.[19]

A large war chest of campaign contributions discourages the development of opposition candidates, either in the primary or the general election, so it is in the interest of powerful incumbents to continue to store up campaign funds—both for their *in terrorem* effect on possible challengers and for use if opposition nevertheless develops. The enormous contributions of the members of both parties to their campaign committees suggest how much surplus funding they actually collect. In other words, campaign contributions are generally collected most easily by those who do not need them, and are most difficult to find for those who do.

Much of the impetus for campaign finance reform has come from people who are appalled by the enormous amount of money spent on political campaigns. We are not among this group; campaign spending ultimately informs an electorate who have many more important things to do in their daily lives than to pay close attention to political campaigns months before the election. However, it is also clear that hard-won campaign contributions could be better used, and used more efficiently, if they were allocated by a political party with a national perspective. Thus, instead of campaign funds piling up in the war chests of incumbents who are bound to be reelected in any event, they would be employed by a party to aid candidates who have the greatest likelihood of winning.

This efficient use of campaign funds is not possible in the current candidate-centered system. Although well-financed incumbents can contribute funds to their party or party campaign committees, the limits on party financing of campaigns hamper the usefulness of these funds. Only tiny percentages of the total amount taken in by Senate or House incumbents can be used on a coordinated expenditure basis to fund the campaigns of deserving challengers or the few underfunded incumbents. Only ending the restriction on party financing of candidates will permit campaign funds from all sources to be used for maximum effectiveness in electing candidates.

Empowering consultants, raising campaign costs, and reducing the policy significance of campaigns. For those who complain that campaigns are too expensive and are not about anything but winning, there is no need to look further than the rise of consultants and professional campaign managers for an adequate explanation. With the decline of the political parties, candidates have had to hire outside consultants to perform the technical tasks that mass market electioneering requires. As David Dulio and Candice Nelson explain:

> Because candidates could no longer depend on party activity to convey their messages, as they once had, candidates began to take advantage of the new technologies that were available to them. Television, the innovation in electioneering that has had by far the biggest impact on campaigns, allowed candidates to take their cases directly to the people. However, the new technology brought with it the need for new skills to apply that technology. The use of television required know-how in areas of production, scriptwriting, editing, and other sophisticated and technical techniques. Candidates and their campaign managers rarely had the skills necessary to create television advertisements, so campaigns turned to those who did—political consultants.[20]

But the decline of the parties and the rise of consultants are outgrowths of the same policy. They both came about because of the forced separation of parties from campaigns—made necessary by the stringent FECA restrictions on parties' financing of or coordination with their candidates. Without the assistance of parties, candidates are required to engage consultants for tasks in the modern campaign that candidates cannot do for themselves. These include developing ads, buying TV time, engaging and instructing the right pollster, and settling on a strategy and "message" suitable for the constituencies they are seeking to attract. There is nothing about these tasks that made them impractical or impossible for parties. If they had been permitted to do so, parties would have employed permanent staff with all these skills and more, and made them available for their candidates at considerably less cost.

The decline of the parties and the corresponding rise of the political consultant also changed the nature of campaigns. Where campaigns were once about policy issues—from meeting the needs of constituents to meeting a foreign threat—the advent of consultants as key players in campaigns often changed the focus simply to winning. Winning was what consultants required in order to attract clients in the future. The role of the campaign consultant is captured in caricature in the 1972 film *The Candidate*. In the film, Robert Redford is a handsome young reformer running for the Senate under the guidance of his unprincipled campaign consultant, Marvin Lucas, played by Peter Boyle. Lucas's goal is to win, and gradually Redford's ideals are stripped away until he is nothing but a good-looking young man with a great smile, ultimately standing for nothing. In the end, he wins the election, and as the media pound on the door of his hotel room hoping for an interview, he turns to his consultant and asks, "Marvin . . . What do we do now?"

The essential truth of the film is that in the atomized electoral process created by a candidate-centric campaign finance system, where campaigns of necessity have to be financed by candidate fundraising and run by outside consultants, there is strong pressure to make the election about nothing more than victory. It may not be an exaggeration to say that the vicious and personality-driven campaigns of today—where issues play a secondary role—are an artifact of the candidate-centered campaign finance system that was adopted in the early 1970s.

Reducing useful information for voters. In *Buckley v. Valeo*, as noted earlier, the Supreme Court held that money was essential for speech. This is obviously true, because political speech can have an impact only if it is disseminated, and dissemination has to be financed in some way. The purpose of political speech, of course, is to inform voters. There can be no government control over the speech produced and disseminated, and happily the

Supreme Court has struck down or undermined some of the provisions in the BCRA that limited when certain kinds of speech could be employed; but any campaign finance reform should aim to assure that the speech reaching voters is as useful as possible. One of the most consistent complaints about today's political campaigns is that they are failing in this respect, that negative and personal attacks have supplanted discussion of the national issues that should be important to voters.

There can be a great deal of debate about what is useful information for voters, but certainly one of the most important elements of any campaign should be providing voters with a sense of what the election of a candidate will mean in terms of national policies. In a candidate-centric system this becomes very difficult. The incentives for candidates who are raising funds separately from their parties is to minimize their party relationship—and their relationship to party policies—in order to maximize their fundraising possibilities and thus their electability. This process tends to emphasize the differences between groups and regions rather than create a national program for which anyone— certainly individual members of Congress, but also political parties—can be held responsible. Even more important, it deprives voters of the most vital kind of information—the relationship between their vote for a particular candidate and its effect on the national policies ultimately adopted by Congress.

Enhancing the power of the "special interests." In *FEC v. Wisconsin Right to Life, Inc.*, the Supreme Court invalidated a BCRA restriction that banned issue ads by nonparty groups within thirty days of a primary election and sixty days of a general election.[21] As much as it is to be welcomed as protecting freedom of speech, the decision nevertheless frees special interest groups to exercise an even more powerful voice in elections than in the past. We believe that the aspersions routinely cast on "special interests" by the media (itself a "special interest") are generally misplaced. We are a nation of special interests, and one of the roles of a democracy is to settle peacefully the many differences in interests among a nation's citizens. However, agreeing that there is nothing illegitimate or antidemocratic about special interests is not the same as asserting that all groups in society represent equally broad constituencies. Political parties represent one of the broadest constituencies in society, and to the extent that the power of political parties is reduced, the power of the special interests is enhanced.

As it is currently structured, our campaign finance law limits the ability of political parties to defend their candidates against attack, but leaves the special interests free—as long as they operate independently of the candidates—to urge voters to support or oppose particular candidates. Nor do parties, without the ability to finance their candidates, have the leverage necessary to develop a set of policies and programs with a national perspective in order to counter the arguments of those pressing the case of special or narrower interests.

As a result, the candidate-centered campaign finance system in the United States makes candidates more susceptible to special interest pressures. Candidates want to avoid attacks from these groups in the future, they want to prevent the financing of their opponents' campaign by these interests, and they want to retain the option in the future to raise their own campaign funds from these groups and from individuals who are sympathetic to them. In this way, the special interests gain greater power over candidates and lawmakers than they would have if there were a separate and independent source of disinterested funding for campaigns—such as a political party.

Finally, special interests are relatively more empowered than more broadly representative groups such as political parties because they have specific prescriptions for action, while parties do not. Something beats nothing every time, and parties cannot develop and advance specific programs because they can rarely get a consensus from the candidates, who must raise campaign funds on their own. There is little interest among candidates in offending anyone or any group that might be a source of campaign support or that might be willing to support an opponent. Thus parties are virtually silent while special interests have loud and persistent voices in our election campaigns. This, too, lends special interests additional power to advance issues they favor and delay actions they oppose.

Implementation of a Better System

Of the many objectives that could be achieved by a well-designed campaign finance system, the current system achieves none. It enhances the advantages of incumbents; favors the choice of wealthy candidates; creates at least the appearance of corruption or undue influence; allocates campaign funds inefficiently; encourages expensive campaigns run by outside consultants; burdens lawmakers with fundraising chores that distract them from their legislative duties; discourages qualified people from running for office; reduces the information on national policy options available to voters; allows special interests to speak more loudly on public issues than the political parties that represent more general interests; and does nothing to develop or refine the political or programmatic choices for American voters.

Under these circumstances, a total overhaul of a failed system would seem to be required, but in fact only one major change in current law is necessary: the elimination of all restrictions on the ability of political parties to finance the campaigns of their candidates. As we show in chapter 3, that single change would go a long way toward addressing all the deficiencies of the current campaign finance system, especially because the parties would become the principal fundraising and expenditure vehicles for most candidates.

Although we might favor the elimination of most contribution and expenditure limits in the current campaign finance law—and the replacement of limits by an effective system of disclosure—the benefits associated with the change in party financing rules would be so significant in our view that there would be no need to undertake still broader reform, or to fight the political battles that complete abandonment of the current system would entail. To be sure, there will be substantial opposition even to the single change we propose; the advantage that the current system offers to incumbents is a powerful incentive for many in Congress to oppose eliminating restrictions on party financing of candidates. But that only means that it makes sense to argue for the narrowest possible reform with the broadest possible impact. Legislation that would remove the limits on parties' financing of their own candidates was actually introduced in both the House (HR 1316, June 15, 2005) and the Senate (S 1091, April 11, 2007). Neither bill was ever voted on in the Senate or the House.

The changes we propose will make elections for the House and Senate more competitive, but there is much they will not do. Even if, as we expect, parties become more involved in the policy process, the structure of our constitutional system will continue to assert itself. The president and Congress will, from time to time, be controlled by different parties, as will the two houses of Congress. There is no indication that American voters will adopt straight-ticket voting, and thus enhance party loyalty as an element of our politics—although if parties are able to develop and implement popular reforms the competition between them in this respect will certainly have some effect on voting habits.

In addition, in a country as large and diverse as the United States, latitude must be left for the expression of many different views through the electoral system. That means that any reform must permit candidates to raise their own funds if they choose to do so, and to remain completely independent of party pressure coming through a party-dominated system of campaign finance.

That said, we believe that several other changes in campaign finance law would help to support a party-centric campaign finance system. Under current law, individuals are limited to an *aggregate* contribution—to political parties and candidates—of slightly more than $100,000 (the amount is indexed for inflation) in any two-year election cycle, with a sublimit of $61,400 (indexed) for contributions to a political party and another sub-limit of $37,500 for contributions to PACs and state/local party accounts used to support federal candidates. This structure is consistent with the candidate-centric fundraising system because it allows individuals to contribute up to the aggregate limit to candidates, but places sublimits (within the overall $100,000 limit) on individual contributions to parties and PACs.

We would modify these rules so that in any two-year cycle individuals could contribute to national parties and party committees 100 percent of the total amount allowable for individuals, parties, and PACs. In other words, we would abolish the indexed $61,400 sublimit on contributions to parties, but would retain the sublimits for PACs and state/local party federal support. The effect of this change would be to increase contributions to parties, by maintaining a limit on contributions to PACs and state/local party committees. To further encourage contributions to parties, we would place a sublimit of 25 percent on the allowable amount that could be contributed directly to candidates. This would reverse the current system, and encourage contributions to parties rather than candidates, while still leaving room for contributions to individual candidates.

There is no comparable aggregate limit for contributions by PACs, although PACs are limited to $5,000 in contributions to candidates and $15,000 to parties per year. We would leave the $5,000 per candidate limit in place (indexed), but increase to $250,000 (indexed) the limit for PAC contributions to parties. In order to encourage PACs to contribute to parties instead of candidates, we would place a sublimit of $100,000 on PAC contributions to candidates.

These changes will redirect the flow of contributions to parties instead of candidates, but will still enable candidates to resist party pressure if they choose and to solicit funds from PACs as well as individuals. However, individual and PAC contributions to candidates will reduce the amount available to contribute to parties in any election cycle, and vice versa.

This competition between the parties and their candidates for contributions does not appear to us a bad thing. If the aggregate limit on contributions to both candidates and parties is set high enough, we believe, the amount ultimately available to parties will be sufficient to provide for the funding of all political campaigns that parties believe their candidates have a chance to win. Parties should also have an incentive to maximize their contributions, even if that means competing with their candidates; and candidates who wish to remain independent should be required to make clear why their independence is of value to their contributors.

The new role we predict for parties of course raises the question of whether parties will begin to dictate officeholders' positions—that is, whether parties, using their new-found clout with candidates, will impose a draconian requirement for party loyalty on all votes in Congress. We believe this is highly unlikely. The first interest of parties is in gaining control and keeping control of government through electing legislative majorities. Under these circumstances, they are not going to commit political suicide by insisting on party loyalty on every vote, especially where that vote might cost the party a seat in the next election. The likelihood is that the party, working with the party's leaders in Congress, will use the same strategy that has always been used by party leaders themselves in both Houses. That is, if the party has the votes to pass the legislation, and sometimes even if it does not, the leaders let some lawmakers vote against the party's position in order to assist them in their re-election efforts. This is likely to be the position of the party in all cases.

Of course, a party will not retain its majority if it wins control of the House or Senate but does not then attempt to implement—at least in substantial part—the platform on which its candidates ran. This is the heart of the quandary faced by all political parties. Except for rigidly ideological parties, the purpose of the party is to govern—otherwise its ideas have no practical value. There is little reason to believe that broad-based inclusive parties like the Republicans and Democrats would sacrifice seats in the House or the Senate in order to achieve rigid ideological objectives. It is more likely that the party and its leaders in Congress would do everything in their power to achieve two main and frequently conflicting goals—maintaining a majority in Congress and implementing the program through which the party attained that control. This issue is discussed more fully in chapter 3.

1

How the Current Campaign Finance System Works For Incumbents and Against Parties

The last chapter offered an overview of the problems associated with the current candidate-centered system of campaign finance in the United States. In this chapter, we look in detail at two of these problems, the way the system favors incumbents and the way it works against parties. Specifically, we make the following observations about our campaign finance laws:

- Virtually every major element of the campaign finance "reforms" adopted since 1971—although adopted under the guise of cleaning up politics and reducing the appearance of corruption—was intended instead to place obstacles in the paths of challengers and thus to favor incumbents.

- Although several of the most egregious and transparent efforts to favor incumbents were struck down by the Supreme Court, the incumbent-protective provisions that remain—primarily the limits placed on party spending in coordination with candidates—are still a significant obstacle to a competitive electoral system in which a challenger can offer a serious threat to an incumbent.

- Finally, even if the political parties were given the authority they need to contribute to and otherwise support their candidates, they are still compelled to defend themselves and their candidates with "hard money" (funds raised from contributions limited as to source and amount), while many of the outside groups that oppose them are able to raise and expend funds without any restriction, and in most cases without any disclosure.

23

The Campaign Finance System and Incumbent Protection

It may come as a surprise to most supporters of campaign finance reform that Congress has been helping itself all these years—rather than trying seriously to clean up the system—but that is the unavoidable conclusion one must draw from a review of what Congress initially proposed as campaign finance reform. Many of these sallies were ultimately struck down by the Supreme Court, mostly because they were transparently pro-incumbent and thus invalid under the First Amendment, and they are not much known or remarked upon today. But the fact that Congress adopted them says a great deal about motives, and casts justifiable doubt on the restrictions that remain. Indeed, the history of modern campaign finance laws has consisted largely of efforts to dress up incumbent protection to look like something more praiseworthy. Although the Supreme Court has said that the danger of corruption or its appearance is the only permissible justification for the free-speech restrictions on campaign giving and spending, Congress has tried to justify campaign finance laws as efforts to prevent "undue influence" or to "level the playing field" or to "equalize political opportunity." But the evidence of lawmakers' real purpose is powerful, and it is clear that putting Congress in charge of campaign finance is like letting the home team pick the referee and write the rules.

Rather than a system that maximizes competition and encourages political accountability, our campaign finance regime is a complex tangle of laws, rules, regulations, exceptions, exemptions, and safe harbors—a veritable labyrinth of federal statutes and regulations spanning 165 pages of the United States Code Annotated and over 300 pages of implementing regulations, and augmented by literally thousands of rulings and interpretations by the FEC.[1] It is difficult to believe that such a system could be consistent with the simple language of the Constitution's First Amendment: "Congress shall make no law . . . abridging the freedom of speech, or of the press; or the right of the people peaceably to assemble, and to petition the Government for a redress of grievances." What could the framers have had in mind with this language, other than a guarantee of freedom to speak in the context of democratic elections?

Moreover, the highly complex campaign finance regime that Congress has created can be a dangerous place to operate without legal counsel. To cite just one example, a key concept in campaign finance regulation is "coordination." Activities "coordinated" with a candidate or campaign are treated as highly regulated contributions, while independent activities (those that are not "coordinated") are largely free of such restraints. Thus, a finding of "coordination" where it should not have occurred can make the difference between free speech and a felony. The FEC regulations defining "coordination" span eight densely printed pages of the Code of Federal Regulations[2] and were recently the subject of a thirty-six-page federal appellate decision in *Shays v. FEC*, which held that the regulations would once again have to be rewritten because they were more lenient than Congress intended.[3] This is not simply a technical point. The amount that parties can spend in coordination with their candidates is strictly limited, but spending on uncoordinated activities is not limited at all. Thus the broader the definition of coordination, the less involved a party can be in a campaign. Accordingly, when the court in the *Shays* case found that the existing rules were too lenient, it was helping Congress reduce the scope of what political parties can do on behalf of their candidates. A decision like this mostly impedes challengers and aids incumbents, because challengers are far more in need of party assistance than incumbents. Once again, incumbents in Congress can be seen making life easier for themselves.

That the real purpose of campaign finance rules is to protect incumbents should be no surprise. First, of course, incumbents are the ones who write the rules, giving them an opportunity to stack the deck in their favor. In almost any other aspect of public life, this inherent conflict of interest would be recognized, and the resulting action viewed through this lens. But surprisingly little commentary about the federal campaign finance laws—FECA in 1971, the 1974 amendments to FECA, and BCRA in 2002, or "McCain-Feingold"—has addressed this obvious issue when considering the legitimacy of these rules.[4]

Second, a close look at those laws makes clear their real purpose. As we will show, almost every key provision of those laws seems to have been designed to benefit and entrench incumbents. Spending limits and contribution limits—the keystones of all modern campaign finance "reforms"—are both of great assistance to incumbents; they reduce the amount of money that challengers can raise and spend and thus magnify the advantages of incumbency. These advantages include, among many others, appropriated funds for staffs, free communications to the state or district, constituent services, name recognition, access to and coverage from local media, and backing from interest groups eager to aid and support an incumbent who has the power to help or harm them.

The proof of the incumbency-protective nature of campaign finance limits is there in the numbers. Since the enactment of the FECA in the early 1970s, the reelection rate of congressional incumbents has increased steadily, and in the last twenty years it has often reached more than 98 percent.[5] Similarly, the amount of money raised by challengers has, relatively speaking, declined, so that the incumbent-to-challenger funding ratio, which was 3 to 2 before FECA, has increased to approximately 5 to 1.[6] So the result of greater campaign finance controls, supposedly passed to "level the playing field," has been to entrench incumbents and *enhance* their fundraising advantage over challengers.

Because many of the inherent advantages of incumbency cannot be eliminated—they are a part of the important process of communication between an officeholder and his constituents—a truly competitive system should at least provide the potential for challengers to spend *more* than incumbents in elections. The place where limits pinch most is precisely in the competitive elections where challengers—if they are allowed to raise and spend sufficient funds to mount an effective campaign against an incumbent—have a decent prospect of winning.

If challengers are to have at least the potential to raise more funds than incumbents, where are these funds to come from? Under the current campaign finance regime, contribution limits make it much more difficult for challengers to raise funds than incumbents; indeed, the gap between incumbent and challenger fundraising is widening. The only logical and consistent source of challenger funding is the political party. Parties alone have the ability and the incentive to provide to challengers the early funding—and the necessary financial support overall—that will give them a chance to overcome the inherent advantages of incumbents. Accordingly, if our goal is a more competitive electoral system, restrictions on parties, more than any other element of our current campaign finance structure, must be eliminated. Only through this change in policy can we be assured of a competitive electoral system in the future.

A Century of "Reform"

During the twentieth century, Congress made several significant efforts to control campaign funding, but every regulatory effort spawned efforts to skirt those limitations, resulting in more and more regulations in an ever increasing downward spiral of complexity. The mind-bending complexity of current law—after years of laws and regulations intended to deal with evasions—is illustrated by the following three tables that appear on the FEC Web site and that are intended to outline the key features of the current federal campaign finance law: contribution limits and party "coordinated" expenditures. They deal generally with contributions to and expenditures by candidates, political parties, and political action committees.

For example, consider table 1-1, which represents the bewildering array of different contribution limits under the FECA:

Table 1-1
Contribution Limits, 2007–8

	To Each Candidate or Candidate Committee per Election	To National Party Committee per Calendar Year	To State, District, & Local Party Committee per Calendar Year	To Any Other Political Committee per Calendar Year[a]	Special Limits
Permissible Individual Contribution	$2,300[b]	$28,500[b]	$10,000 (combined limit)	$5,000	$108,200[b] overall biennial limit: • $42,700[b] to all candidates • $65,500[b] to all PACs and parties[c]
Permissible National Party Committee Contribution	$5,000	No limit	No limit	$5,000	$39,900[b] to Senate candidate per campaign[d]
Permissible State, District, & Local Party Committee Contribution	$5,000 (combined limit)	No limit	No limit	$5,000 (combined limit)	No limit
Permissible PAC Contribution (multicandidate[e])	$5,000	$15,000	$5,000 (combined limit)	$5,000	No limit
Permissible PAC Contribution (not multicandidate)	$2,300[b]	$28,500[b]	$10,000 (combined limit)	$5,000	No limit
Permissible Authorized Campaign Committee Contribution	$2,000[f]	No limit	No limit	$5,000	No limit

SOURCE: Federal Election Commission, "Contribution Limits 2007–08," http://www.fec.gov/pages/brochures/contriblimits.shtml.
NOTES: a. A contribution earmarked for a candidate through a political committee counts against the original contributor's limit for that candidate. In certain circumstances, the contribution may also count against the contributor's limit to the PAC. See 11 CFR 110.6; see also 11 CFR 110.1(h); b. These contribution limits are increased for inflation in odd-numbered years; c. No more than $42,700 of this amount may be contributed to state and local party committees and PACs; d. This limit is shared by the national committee and the Senate campaign committee; e. A multicandidate committee is a political committee with more than fifty contributors which has been registered for at least six months and, with the exception of state party committees, has made contributions to five or more candidates for federal office. See 11 CFR 100.5(e)(3); f. A federal candidate's authorized committee(s) may contribute no more than $2,000 per election to another federal candidate's authorized committee(s). See 2 U.S.C. 432(e)(3)(B).

The crucial rules governing coordinated party expenditures are similarly complex, as tables 1-2 and 1-3, also taken from the FEC Web site, make clear. Table 1-3 even refers the reader to yet another link to another table to help explicate the various restrictions and conditions in the law.

Table 1-2

AUTHORITY TO MAKE COORDINATED PARTY EXPENDITURES ON BEHALF OF HOUSE, SENATE, AND PRESIDENTIAL NOMINEES

Type of Party Committee	Authority
National Party Committee	May make expenditures on behalf of House, Senate, and presidential nominees. May authorize[a] other party committees to make expenditures against its own spending limits. Shares limits with national congressional and senatorial campaign committees.
State Party Committee	May make expenditures on behalf of House and Senate nominees seeking election in the committee's state. May authorize[a] other party committees to make expenditures against its own spending limits. May be authorized[a] by national committee to make expenditures on behalf of presidential nominee that count against the national committee's limit.
Local Party Committee	May be authorized[a] by national or state party committee to make expenditures against its limits.

SOURCE: Federal Election Commission, "2008 Coordinated Party Expenditure Limits," http://www.fec.gov/info/charts_441ad.shtml.
NOTE: a. The authorizing committee must provide prior authorization specifying the amount the committee may spend.

Table 1-3

CALCULATING 2008 COORDINATED PARTY EXPENDITURE LIMITS

Nominee	Amount	Formula
Presidential Nominee	$19,151,200	2 cents x state VAP x COLA
Senate Nominee	Various; see Federal Election Committee, "Coordinated Party Expenditure Limits for 2008 Senate Nominees," http://www.fec.gov/info/charts_441ad.shtml	The greater of: $20,000 x COLA or 2 cents x state VAP x COLA
House Nominee in State with Only One Representative	$84,100	$20,000 x COLA
House Nominee in Other States	$42,100	$10,000 x COLA
Nominee for Delegate or Resident Commissioner	$42,100	$10,000 x COLA

SOURCE: Federal Election Commission, "2008 Coordinated Party Expenditure Limits," http://www.fec.gov/info/charts_441ad.shtml.
NOTES: VAP = voting age population. COLA = cost-of-living adjustment. The 2008 COLA is 4.25; limits are rounded to the nearest hundred. Delegates are elected in American Samoa, the District of Columbia, Guam, and the Virgin Islands; a resident commissioner is elected in Puerto Rico.

As if this were not complicated enough, there is an entirely additional set of rules governing "independent expenditures," "electioneering communications," and "issue advocacy" by parties, as well as by outside individuals and groups such as labor unions, corporations, so-called Section 527 organizations, and various nonprofits and tax-exempt groups. Those different rules are so complex that they do not easily lend themselves to graphic depiction. But here's a stab, nonetheless:

Table 1-4
RULES GOVERNING INDEPENDENT AND RELATED CAMPAIGN SPENDING BY INDIVIDUALS, ORGANIZATIONS, PARTIES, AND OTHER ENTITIES

	Independent Expenditure (Express Advocacy re Candidate)	Electioneering Communication (Broadcast during Election Season; Functional Equivalent of Express Advocacy)	Issue Advocacy	Get-Out-the-Vote
Individuals	Unlimited; disclosure required[a]	Unlimited; disclosure required	Unregulated	Unregulated
PACs	Unlimited if not coordinated; disclosure required	Unlimited; disclosure required	Unlimited; disclosurerequired	Unlimited; disclosure required
Parties	Unlimited if "independent"; limited if coordinated; disclosure required	Unlimited; disclosure required	Unlimited; disclosure required	Unlimited; disclosure required
Corporations, Unions	Prohibited except for internal communications	Prohibited	Unregulated	Unregulated
Nonprofit Ideological Corporations	Allowed if no corporation or union $; disclosure required	Allowed if no corporation or union $; disclosure required	Unregulated	Unregulated
501 (c)(3) Traditional Charity	Prohibited	Prohibited	Unregulated	Unregulated
501(c)(4) Social Welfare, (5) Labor, (6) Business Organization	Some candidate advocacy allowed if not primary purpose; limited disclosure required	Some candidate advocacy allowed if not primary purpose; limited disclosure required	Unregulated (subject to primary purpose test)	Unregulated (subject to primary purpose test)

SOURCE: Authors' interpretations of relevant provisions in Federal Election Campaign Act and the Internal Revenue Code.
NOTE: a. It remains an open question whether groups of individuals pooling their contributions may give unlimited amounts.

Section 527s, depending on whether incorporated or not, can engage in extensive political activity, subject to significant disclosure, but if they employ express advocacy or electing candidates becomes their "major purpose," they can be subject to PAC-type FEC regulation and limitation.[7]

Congressional Action

In *Money Matters: Consequences of Campaign Finance Reform in U.S. House Elections*, three scholars trace the development of restrictions on contributions and expenditures from their earliest beginnings through the FECA Amendments of 1974. The Progressive Era saw the first sustained efforts to limit campaign contributions and expenditures, but to no avail: "The federal reform efforts instituted during the first quarter of the twentieth century were simply unworkable. Corporate contributions were sometimes simply ignored and creative techniques were developed to circumvent the ban on corporate contributions . . . The campaign reporting requirements were essentially useless because the legislation lacked any real enforcement provisions."[8]

A key aim of the early reforms was to counter the divisiveness of parties, partisanship, and special interests. But incumbent officeholders and political interests quickly learned how to turn these good-faith reformist impulses to their advantage, principally by focusing the attention of reformers on the question of corruption, the appearance of corruption, and the costs of campaigns. Thus, although the rationale for many campaign finance reforms in the last century was that they would make our politics fairer and more honest, the reforms have instead made elections less fair by increasing the advantage of incumbents.[9]

Congress began legislating on campaign finance issues in 1907 when, as part of Theodore Roosevelt's progressive reforms, the Tillman Act was passed. The act restricted corporate involvement in politics by prohibiting national banks and corporations from contributing to federal campaigns. The themes sounded and market-tested back then—preventing corruption of the political process by "malefactors of great wealth," and "leveling the playing field" for candidates and citizens—are still with us today. Next came the Federal Corrupt Practices Act of 1925, which provided for disclosure of certain receipts and expenditures.

Although it was a feature of the Progressive movement to weaken the power of the political parties, the most significant restriction on party finances came in the Hatch Act of 1940, which put an overall limit of $3,000,000 on how much national party committees could raise and spend annually, and a $5,000 limit on contributions to them. While other political actors could skirt these restrictions by creating committees that operated in only one state, by multiplying committees, or by operating "independent" committees, the national party committees were stuck with abiding by these limitations. The hydraulic effect of these rules was to decentralize fundraising, moving it away from the national parties and toward candidates, interest groups, and state and local parties, and resulting in relatively weak national party structures and political activities.[10] As we will see, when the more comprehensive campaign finance reform occurred in the early 1970s, it formalized a decentralized, candidate-centric system that had developed as a result of the Hatch Act restrictions.

When these early laws were seen as ineffective in deterring corruption and undue influence—President Lyndon B. Johnson once observed that federal campaign finance law was "more loophole than law"—the demand for campaign finance reform continued.[11] The next major push for reform began after the high-spending, media-focused presidential campaigns of the 1960s.[12] Proposals included limiting campaign spending, curtailing campaign advertising, and providing public financing. Less restrictive proposals involved closing loopholes in reporting and disclosure of campaign funding so that the voters would be better informed about who was supporting which candidates and could use that information at the polls.

The 1960s were a time of great change in the technology of political campaigning. The growth of television made it easier for candidates to reach voters without the aid of political parties. "As new campaign technologies continued to develop and the mass media came of age . . . political parties began to lose much of their traditional financial intermediary role [and] campaigns became candidate-centered."[13] As we note in chapter 4, exactly why this occurred is very unclear. The mere fact that parties were no longer necessary for candidates does not explain why they were shunted aside for fundraising purposes. But by the end of the 1960s candidates themselves began to assume the burdens of raising the necessary funds for their campaigns. The new candidate-centered campaign was more expensive to run because of the high cost of television advertising. This change in technology gave rise to efforts in Congress, beginning in 1969, to impose restrictions on campaign spending, always a popular incumbent-protection measure. The first of these bills, adopted in 1970, imposed spending limits on broadcasting and required broadcasters to sell advertising time to candidates at the lowest commercial rates; the bill was vetoed by President Nixon, and the veto was sustained.[14]

It is significant that the belief behind the legislative efforts of the 1960s was not that campaign finance was giving rise to corruption, but rather that it had become too expensive. The fact that the proposed bills applied equally to incumbents and challengers is, of course, irrelevant. Incumbents have myriad ways to become known to their constituents; challengers generally have only one way—through campaign spending. Equalizing the access of both incumbents and challengers to television advertising was thus a benefit for incumbents. John Samples notes this shift in focus: "Congress radically changed course on campaign finance in 1969. Whereas disclosure, tax subsidies, and liberalized spending limits had dominated the regulatory agenda before 1968, only restrictions on campaign spending passed Congress in 1970. Congress had moved from limited regulation to systematic suppression of spending."[15]

Congress was finally successful in enacting restrictive campaign spending legislation in 1971. In that year, it adopted the Federal Election Campaign Act (FECA), the predecessor law which created the current architecture of campaign finance law. FECA had something for everybody, but virtually all of it ultimately aided incumbents. Incumbents pushed for two novel—and, as it turned out, clearly unconstitutional—provisions: sharply *curtailed* media expenditures and severe limitations on the amount of money that candidates and their fami-lies could contribute to their own campaigns. The limits were $50,000, $35,000, and $25,000, respectively, for candidates for president, Senate, and House. These restrictions had two effects. They relieved the incumbent of the need to raise large amounts of money in order to beat back a wealthy challenger, and they also made it more difficult for challengers to overcome the name recognition enjoyed by incumbents. This is a pattern—benefits for incumbents hidden in what are described as "reforms"—that emerged over and over again as the FECA was amended over time. As to the brand-new media expenditure limits, harmful to challengers, Congressman Morris Udall (D-AZ) remarked shortly after the passage of FECA in 1971, "It brings this television monster under control."[16]

Both parties wanted and got the repeal of the marginally effective limits on party contributions and expenditures enacted in 1940, but by 1971 the parties' fundraising abilities had atrophied so significantly that the temporary lifting of limits produced no spurt of party funding in the 1972 elections.[17] Corporations and unions got a provision legitimizing their PACs—which, of course, was another benefit for incumbents, who normally receive up to eight times as much in campaign contributions from PACs as challengers. Reformers, for their part, got the first truly effective and comprehensive disclosure rules. Though challengers got the ability to raise money more easily from supporters (there was no contribution limit for individuals in the 1971 act), the media limits meant that they could not spend that money in the most effective way.

The new law went into effect before the 1972 elections. However, the limits on broadcast spending and candidates' personal spending alone were not effective in protecting incumbents in the election of 1972. The Democrats, the majority party in both houses of Congress, lost three Senate seats, bringing their Senate majority to fifty-four, and thirteen House seats, bringing their House majority margin to fifty. This loss probably stimulated a desire to tighten the rules for the 1974 election, and the result was the most comprehensive campaign finance reform to that time, the modestly named Federal Election Campaign Act Amendments of 1974.[18] The new law contained an unprecedented set of restrictions on campaign finance activity that went well beyond the Watergate campaign finance abuses they were supposed to correct. The American Civil Liberties Union (ACLU) immediately dubbed the FECA Amendments "an Incumbent Protection Act."[19] Of the fourteen challengers who had beaten sitting senators or representatives in 1972, all of them spent more than was permitted to both incumbents and challengers by the 1974 amendments. Of the challengers who lost in 1972 but garnered at least 45 percent of the vote, half spent more than the limitations later imposed by the 1974 amendments.[20]

The 1974 amendments were extremely strict and far-reaching:

- They imposed severe limitations on the amounts that could be spent by candidates on their political campaigns (retaining the 1971 limits on candidates' use of personal funds), by political parties to support their candidates, and even by individuals and groups that were *independent* of any candidate or campaign.

- They mandated sharp limits on the amount of money that could be given to political candidates ($1,000 from individuals; $5,000 from political committees and political parties; $25,000 total annual federal contributions by individuals).

- They broadened the requirements for disclosure of even small contributions and imposed those rules on groups that merely provided election-year information and discussion about incumbents and candidates in a wholly nonpartisan manner.

- They created a new enforcement agency, the Federal Election Commission (FEC), whose members would be appointed by the same incumbent politicians they were supposed to be regulating.

- They provided for public funding of presidential primary and general election campaigns, but with a number of limitations and restrictions guaranteed to reinforce the status quo.[21]

Under the amended FECA, anyone who sponsored a small newspaper ad criticizing an incumbent president of the United States running for reelection could now be committing a federal crime. Indeed, substantial criminal penalties were prescribed for violation of most of the law's new provisions, almost all of which, as we shall see in a moment, seem clearly designed to enhance the power of incumbency.

At the time many of these restrictions were enacted, the Supreme Court had not ruled on the constitutionality of expenditure or contribution limits. Many commentators believed that regulation of the funding of political activity did not deserve special constitutional scrutiny; they viewed it as the regulation of money rather than the regulation of speech. In its key decision on this question, however, the landmark case of *Buckley v. Valeo*, the Supreme Court held that in politics, money was the equivalent of speech, because money was required to disseminate political speech.[22] In *Buckley*, the Court measured post-Watergate laws, and particularly the 1974 amendments, against the demands of the First Amendment. The resulting decision laid down a number of rules that would govern campaign finance law for the next generation:

- Campaign finance regulations cut to the core of the First Amendment's protections of political speech and association and must be closely scrutinized.

- Campaign contributions and spending are speech within the meaning of the First Amendment.

- Campaign finance may be regulated to prevent corruption or the appearance of corruption, but not to equalize the spending of competing candidates or the influence of different voters or groups, or to limit the resources devoted to campaigns.

- Contributions and expenditures are to be treated differently; expenditures enjoy the highest level of protection, while contributions are less protected and more susceptible to limitation because they more clearly raise the danger of corruption.

- Reporting and disclosure requirements are generally constitutional because they perform the valuable role of informing voters about the sources of the funds used for financing campaign activity, despite their negative effect on political privacy and freedom of association.

- Campaign finance limitations and regulations can be applied only to those activities that expressly advocate the election or defeat of federal candidates, and not to general political speech. The requirement for "express advocacy" excluded from FECA coverage any communications that did not involve asking the voters to vote for or against a particular candidate, and in turn gave rise to the concept of "soft money"—i.e., funds that could be used for many election-related activities but not express advocacy. The only funds that could be used for express advocacy were "hard money"—the contributions subject to FECA's amount and source limitations.

- Public funding of candidates is constitutional, even with limits imposed as a condition of receiving public funds, because such funding may further First Amendment values by facilitating public discussion and electoral communication and reducing the influence of large private contributions.[23]

These "reforms" had an immediate impact on campaigns, summarized as follows by Bradley Smith, a former member of the FEC: "Within a few years of the passage of the 1974 FECA Amendments, strange things began to happen. Incumbent reelection rates began to rise, reaching record levels in the late 1980s and setting off a nationwide craze for term limits. Incumbents actually increased their fundraising advantage over challengers after FECA was passed, from approximately 1.5 to one to more than four to one. Total spending on congressional campaigns continued to rise, by nearly 400 percent from 1976 through 1998, and candidates began to spend more time, rather than less, raising money for campaigns."[24]

As we have been arguing, spending and contribution limits in general have a strongly pro-incumbent flavor, and this is especially true of contribution and spending limits for parties. Incumbents, as noted above, have many ways to advertise themselves to voters while they hold office. This places them at an immediate advantage vis-à-vis challengers, who often start off with no significant name recognition and no substantial funds with which to gain it. The political party is often the only reliable source of the early campaign contributions that can enable a challenger to hire the staff and begin the extensive advertising that alone can introduce him to a congressional district or an entire state. Restricting party contributions or coordinated spending is thus a fairly transparent incumbent-protection tactic.

In concluding that spending was the same thing as speech in the context of political campaigns, and thus that the limits on contributions and expenditures in the 1974 amendments raised substantial issues of free speech under the First Amendment, the Court placed an immense hurdle in the path of incumbents who wished to suppress the campaigns of challengers. In its analysis, the Court gave Congress considerable deference by agreeing that concern about corruption or the appearance of corruption was an acceptable justification for restrictions on campaign contributions and thus on protected speech. However, the Court would not accept any other justification for the restrictions imposed by the 1974 amendments, and therefore concluded that *expenditure* limitations—which were not related to corruption or the appearance of corruption—were unconstitutional. Expenditure limitations for political parties were not addressed, although the Court recognized that expenditure limits in general were favorable to incumbents. A passage in *Buckley* displays the Court's disdain for what Congress was trying to do:

> In this discussion, we address only the argument that the contribution limitations alone impermissibly discriminate against non-incumbents. We do not address the more serious argument that

these limitations, in combination with the limitation on expenditures by individuals and groups, the limitation on a candidate's use of his own personal and family resources, and the overall ceiling on campaign expenditures invidiously discriminate against major-party challengers and minor-party candidates.

Since an incumbent is subject to these limitations to the same degree as his opponent, the Act, on its face, appears to be even-handed. The appearance of fairness, however, may not reflect political reality. Although some incumbents are defeated in every congressional election, it is axiomatic that an incumbent usually begins the race with significant advantages. In addition to the factors of voter recognition and the status accruing to holding federal office, the incumbent has access to substantial resources provided by the Government. These include local and Washington offices, staff support, and the franking privilege. *Where the incumbent has the support of major special-interest groups . . . and is further supported by the media, the overall effect of the contribution and expenditure limitations enacted by Congress could foreclose any fair opportunity of a successful challenge.*[25]

The rights of and restrictions on political parties were not at the center of the *Buckley* Court's attention. The Court did not comment extensively on the fact that political party committees, like PACs, were limited to $5,000 in making contributions to candidates, and the Court suggested that parties would do well because individuals could give them up to the annual federal contribution cap of $25,000.[26] The party expenditure provision, which gave parties some limited exemption from the act's rigid expenditure limits, was not directly at issue in *Buckley*.[27]

The restrictions on parties were ultimately reduced somewhat after *Buckley*. In clean-up amendments to FECA in 1976, Congress increased from $5,000 to $20,000 the amount that individuals could contribute to party committees; it also increased to $15,000 the amount PACs could give to parties and increased to $17,500 the amount that parties could give to senatorial candidates.[28] These were substantial percentage increases, but since senatorial campaigns cost a minimum of several hundred thousand dollars in the late 1970s, an increase to $17,500 didn't—and doesn't—mean much.[29]

The Court's acceptance of contribution limits was good news for incumbents, who do not want to face a well-funded challenger, but the rejection of expenditure limitations for candidates and independent groups must have been unwelcome, even though restrictions on political party expenditures were retained.[30] Coupled with the Court's refusal to allow any limitations on what a person might spend on his own behalf, this left incumbents in a position where they might have to face that well-heeled and well-funded challenger. Other aspects of the Court's decision in *Buckley* must also have been unsettling, particularly the holding that political expenditures were a form of speech—placing them squarely within First Amendment protections. This left incumbents with few options. At one point, there was talk of a constitutional amendment excluding campaign financing restrictions from First Amendment protections, but that was determined to be impractical and maybe even impolitic. Finally, incumbents were likely to have been disturbed by another of the Court's holdings, that FECA restrictions applied only to express advocacy; this gave rise to soft money and the issue ads, which were also inimical to the interests of incumbents and ultimately stimulated the adoption of the Bipartisan Campaign Reform Act (BCRA), the last of the campaign reform measures thus far adopted by Congress.

Let us consider more closely the Court's conclusion that FECA applied only to express advocacy, i.e., to explicit requests that a candidate be elected or defeated. If the strictures of FECA applied only to funds used to advocate a candidate's election or defeat, there remained a wide range of things for which political parties could, without any limitation, collect and use funds. These included activities such as getting out the vote, advertising the party's issue positions, and supporting the party's administrative and physical infrastructure. Because it was exempt from any restrictions, soft money could be contributed to parties by corporations, labor unions, and any other group or individual, in unlimited amounts.

By 1996, it had been discovered that soft money could also be used for "issue advocacy," which in some cases could be as effective as asking voters to vote for or against a particular candidate. In issue advocacy, a particular issue—like gun control—would be the focus of an advertisement, with a statement at the end asking the voter to call a particular candidate and tell him to stop opposing (or favoring) the registration of firearms. Because the ad dealt only with an issue, and did not expressly advocate the election or defeat of a candidate, it was not covered by the 1974 amendments to FECA, but it informed the electorate about the position of a candidate on an issue that might be important to voters.

Thus, with issue ads and soft money, political parties and others had a powerful weapon—outside the restrictions of existing campaign finance laws—for attacking incumbents, who were of course the candidates with issue positions to attack. The threat to incumbents implicit in soft money and issue advocacy was probably a major motivating factor in the enactment of the BCRA. In addition to outlawing soft money contributions to political parties, the BCRA also prohibited election-season broadcast advertising by corporations or unions that even so much as mentioned the name of a federal candidate. In another landmark ruling, *McConnell v. FEC*, a closely divided Supreme Court upheld these major features.[31] The Court majority believed that the large soft money contributions to political parties were an effort to skirt the restrictions on contributions to candidates and carried the same potential for corruption or the appearance of corruption, or at least the potential for undue access and influence. The ban on broadcasting was upheld on the ground that the advertisements were really partisan and political, despite the lack of express advocacy, and that they could be banned if they were sponsored by corporations, unions, or even nonprofit membership organizations like the ACLU.[32]

Incumbent Advantages in the Current Campaign Finance Regime

What, then, is the effect of these various constitutional and statutory interactions on the current landscape of campaign finance regulation? Although the Supreme Court has declared unconstitutional many of the provisions that were most favorable to incumbents, some still remain, particularly contribution limits and restrictions on the ability of parties to finance the campaigns of their candidates. In this section we look at the provisions that were enacted, even though some did not survive Supreme Court review. Our review raises the question of whether there was ever a true attempt to reform campaign finance, or whether Congress simply dressed up its real intentions in the sheep's clothing of reform.

Expenditure limits. Because incumbents begin every election campaign in a position of advantage, they are comforted by expenditure limits. To the extent that they can limit the funds available to a challenger, or the speed with which the challenger can assemble those funds, the incumbent reaps advantages. In principle, the ideal expenditure limit from the incumbent's point of view is anything lower than the amount necessary to run a credible campaign against him. This objective was apparently at work in the FECA law at issue in *Buckley*. It set the expenditure limits for a House election at $70,000, while the average successful challenger's House campaign in previous years had cost approximately double that amount.[33] The significance of a $70,000 limit becomes clear when one realizes that the value of the franking privilege—which members of Congress use extensively to advertise their work for their constituents—was worth $71,300, slightly *more* by itself than the $70,000 allowed for all campaign expenses by challengers. One liberal group estimated that the total direct monetary value of the perquisites of office and benefits provided to incumbents was close to $1,000,000 during a two-year term.[34] On the Senate side, the general election spending limit was twelve cents per citizen of voting age per state, or barely enough to send one letter to each potential voter.

Little wonder, then, that the *Buckley* Court, without hesitation, struck down limitations on campaign expenditures as contrary to the central understanding of the First Amendment—that political speech must be robust, uninhibited, and unrestrained. Limits on campaign expenditures violate this core premise and undermine the competitiveness of elections. As Bradley Smith observes, the most effective way to challenge an incumbent is to run a well-financed campaign not subject to limits; where challengers have been able to do so, their chances of winning have increased dramatically. "Just as a challenger starts to become competitive," Smith notes as well, "campaign spending limits choke off political competition."[35]

Similarly, Rodney Smith, who has held a number of top fundraising positions for national Republican organizations, points out that, between 1992 and 2000, the campaign funds available to a challenger were the most important factor in determining the outcome of House races against incumbents: "Lack of money by challengers, not gerrymandering, was the single biggest reason that the vast majority of House incumbents faced little or no real competition when running for reelection. When challengers raised less than $400,000, as they did in 83 percent of all House campaigns against incumbents, the incumbent won an unbelievable 99 percent of the races. . . .

When challengers raised more than $1 million, incumbents won only 71 percent of the time."[36]

In the FECA Amendments, Congress restricted the effectiveness of the financial resources available to challengers in four ways: limiting the size of contributions, limiting overall campaign expenditures, limiting expenditures paid from the candidate's own funds, and limiting expenditures by independent groups supporting or opposing candidates. In *Buckley*, the Court approved contribution limits, but rejected all mandatory spending limits, and it has maintained this position consistently ever since, holding most recently that there is no justification for mandatory expenditure limits that will have the inevitable effect of suppressing political speech and electoral competition.[37] Nevertheless, incumbents keep trying to limit the financial resources of challengers, and continue to probe for methods for doing so that are within the constitutional boundaries set by the Supreme Court.

For example, in *Buckley*, the Supreme Court declared that candidates have a constitutional right to spend as much as they want on their own candidacy: "The First Amendment simply cannot tolerate [statutory] restriction[s] upon the freedom of a candidate to speak without legislative limit on behalf of his own candidacy."[38] The one exception to this principle approved by the Court was a "voluntary" limit agreed to as a condition for receiving government funding for a campaign. The Court used this rationale to uphold expenditure limits on presidential candidates who accept the public funding made available for their campaigns by the FECA Amendments. But the Court's position on a candidate's freedom to finance his own campaign placed all incumbents in jeopardy. Although most of the sources of campaign funds for challengers had been narrowed, the possibility of a wealthy challenger now could not be excluded.

This gave rise to the ingenious "Millionaire Amendment," which was added to the BCRA as an incumbent-protecting sweetener. Its obvious purpose was to counter the impact of a self-financed candidate for Congress by stipulating that in any House race in which one candidate contributes more than $350,000 to his own campaign, the other candidate will be entitled to an increase in *contribution* limits of *three times* the normal amount; under a slightly different formula, favored Senate candidates could get a six-fold increase in the contribution limits in their races. Though seemingly neutral, in that it applied to all candidates and opponents, this provision was clearly designed and justified as an incumbent-protection measure, providing a last line of defense to safeguard incumbents from challenges by a well-funded opponent.[39] Campaign finance data show that incumbents almost never have to spend any significant amount of their own money to gain reelection. For example, between 1992 and 2000, the personal funds spent by challengers averaged $50,811, while incumbents spent only $10,023.[40] The Millionaire Amendment also cynically undermined the very rationale for contribution limits: by raising the contribution limits so substantially, it allowed an incumbent facing a high-spending, self-financed challenger to be even more "corruptly influenced."[41]

But this amendment was not the only effort by Congress to circumvent Supreme Court rulings and protect incumbents. Apparently fearing that FEC regulations might not sufficiently inhibit political parties from coordinating their putatively independent spending with their candidates, Congress in the BCRA adopted a provision that required parties to choose between limited coordinated and unlimited uncoordinated spending to support their nominees. The Court handily determined that this statutory extortion did not pass constitutional muster.[42] Since parties had a constitutional right to speak independently on behalf of their candidates, they could not be penalized for exercising that right through denial of their right to coordinate expenditures with that candidate at some earlier or later point. Congress could not make parties give up their right to speak in order to exercise their right to associate. As a result of this ruling and of the elimination of party soft money, "independent expenditures" by parties on behalf of their candidates, especially on the Democratic side, climbed significantly in 2004.[43]

Finally, what incumbents dread almost as much as a well-financed challenger is a well-financed independent group or individual who will speak out against them during the election season. From the very beginning, Congress has tried to use the campaign finance laws to take aim at this classic form of First Amendment activity as well. The original FECA contained limits on media expenditures by independent groups or individuals "on behalf of" or "in derogation of" any political candidate, even if the speaker had nothing to do with the candidate.[44] Courts quickly struck those provisions down as violations of First Amendment principles. Similarly, the sweeping 1974 amendments contained an extraordinary stipulation that prohibited even persons or groups who had nothing to do with a candidate from spending more than

$1,000 *in an entire calendar year* on activities or communications "relative to" a candidate.[45] It did not take long for the *Buckley* Court to invalidate this limitation on independent speech, which "heavily burdens core First Amendment expression."[46] In the discussion below of the BCRA's treatment of soft money and issue ads, we will again see incumbents using legislation to suppress unwanted criticism originating with the political parties.

Contribution limits. Contribution limits also favor incumbents. The lower the limits, the harder it is for challengers to raise funds to run an effective campaign. While incumbents are subject, on paper, to the same limits as challengers, by virtue of incumbency alone they have a much larger Rolodex of contributors and much more ready access to the interest groups who are only too happy to support an incumbent politician, particularly one who sits on a committee in their area of interest. Contribution limits help maintain the status quo, since the forces of change have often relied on a few financial angels to enhance their ability to communicate their message.[47] Eugene McCarthy's insurgent campaign against Lyndon Johnson in 1968 and Ross Perot's self-financed campaign in 1992 are both examples of the importance of contribution limits in suppressing challengers. McCarthy was bankrolled by a few liberals when there were no contribution limits, and Perot financed himself after the Supreme Court declared that there could be no limits on a candidate's contribution to his own campaign.

Despite the force of these arguments, the Court turned them aside in *Buckley* and upheld limits on contributions to federal candidates by individuals ($1,000) and political action committees ($5,000) and on overall annual federal personal contributions ($25,000). This decision made life easier for incumbents and harder for challengers, especially because this cap on individual contributions to candidates is still one-size-fits-all, with no differentiation or gradation between amounts that can be given to presidential, senatorial, or congressional candidates, despite the very different levels of expenditures which the campaigns require.

Finally, the BCRA increased the limit on contributions to candidates from $1,000 to $2,000, but since inflation makes that limit the equivalent of about $500 in 1976 dollars, the net effect was a 50 percent reduction in the federal contribution limit, making fundraising more difficult for challengers than it was in 1976. However, the new limit is indexed for inflation, which at least means that it will not continue to decline in value. The BCRA also increased to $57,000 the amount that can be given to national political parties, and to $95,000 the total that each individual can contribute nationally to federal politics in a two-year cycle; each of these figures was also indexed for inflation. But since parties are unable to spend their resources efficiently by contributing to or coordinating expenditures with their candidates, the additional funds they can raise through these higher limits are a lot less effective than they might be in helping challengers. Contributions to political committees other than party committees remained capped at $5,000 per year, as table 1-1 indicates.

Incumbent protection through contribution limits is not the objective of Congress alone. Many state legislatures have adopted the same idea. Recently, for example, the Court struck down a set of state contribution limits that were so low—$400 for governor, $300 for state senator, $200 for state assemblyman, and limits of the same size on contributions by a political party to each of its candidates—and so protective of incumbents that they violated First Amendment standards. "Contribution limits that are too low," the Court held, "can . . . harm the electoral process by preventing challengers from mounting effective campaigns against incumbent officeholders, thereby reducing democratic accountability."[48]

At the state and local level, in fact, we find a lot of variation in contribution limits, including many cases in which there are *no limits* on contributions to candidates by individuals or political parties, or both. States without limits include Alabama, California, Illinois, Indiana, Iowa, Louisiana, Mississippi, Nebraska, New Mexico, North Carolina, North Dakota, Oregon, Pennsylvania, South Dakota, Texas, Utah, Vermont, Virginia, and Wyoming.[49] Given that there are states with extremely high contribution ceilings, like New York, as well as states with none at all, and given that there is no evident or prevalent pattern of corruption in those no-limit states, it is difficult to argue that low contribution limits such as exist at the federal level are necessary to insure good and honest government, or a government perceived as good and honest.[50] Indeed, a study published in March 2007 by the Pew Charitable Trusts shows that Utah and Virginia, two states with some of the least restrictive laws on campaign finance, were judged to be at the top of the list of best-governed states, while many of the other states with relatively unrestrictive campaign finance laws—Texas, Iowa, North Dakota, and Pennsylvania among others—

ranked favorably.[51] This is not the anomaly that some might think. High or no limits on contribution with full and timely disclosure not only helps challengers, but it creates the possibility of changes in party control that can reveal corruption by the former party that held control. It is when virtually all incumbents are reelected, and there is little chance for the minority to become the majority, that corruption is most likely to be swept under the rug. In that case, the minority settles for the crumbs that the majority provides instead of seeking to become the majority itself.

Coordinated expenditures. Expenditures that are coordinated with a candidate or a campaign are treated as though they are contributions to that campaign, and are subject to the same restrictions and limitations as contributions. However, national political parties were granted a dispensation by law to coordinate campaign expenditures with their candidates—$42,100 for House candidates ($84,100 for one-district states) and $84,100 to $2,284,900, depending on the voting population of the state, for Senate candidates (the odd numbers are because the amounts are indexed each year for inflation). Given the costs of winning campaigns today—the mean successful House race in 2006 cost $1.26 million, and the mean successful Senate race $8.84 million—party coordinated expenditures are a drop in the bucket.[52] In addition, parties' independent and uncoordinated spending on behalf of their candidates is likely to be spent inefficiently, and in many cases counterproductively. For example, in hearings on Senate Bill 1091, a bill to eliminate restrictions on party coordinated spending, several Senators engaged in a colloquy with a witness about whether it was possible to "pull down" an uncoordinated political party ad that was damaging the candidate's campaign.[53]

As might be expected, the boundary between coordinated and uncoordinated expenses is yet another area where the incumbent-protective nature of the campaign finance laws becomes glaringly apparent. Although the 1974 amendments attempted to limit independent expenditures by anyone on behalf of candidates—a clear incumbent-protective device—the relevant provision was struck down by the Supreme Court as an obvious interference with free speech. The rules for independent or uncoordinated expenditures by political parties, however, were not clear until 1996, when—in the case of *Colorado Republican Federal Campaign Committee v. FEC* (*Colorado Republican I*)— the Supreme Court held that political parties have the same freedom to make independent, i.e., uncoordinated, expenditures on behalf of their candidates as any other person or group.[54]

At that point, it became vitally important to incumbents to make sure that independent expenditures by parties—which were now potentially unlimited—were made as ineffective as possible. In other words, the interest of incumbents was to broaden the definition of when party expenditures were deemed to be coordinated, so that the limitations on the amount of permissible coordinated expenses were not vitiated by ineffective or lax enforcement of the boundary between coordinated and uncoordinated expenditures. For that reason, as noted above, Congress has been vigilant in pushing the FEC to adopt the broadest possible definition of coordination—going so far as to use the BCRA to vacate a rule of the FEC whose definition of coordinated expenses it considered too lenient. This effort assures that there will be as little contact as possible between parties and the campaigns of their candidates on the subject of the party's uncoordinated expenditures. More coordination would make the party's expenditures more effective and thus more troublesome for incumbents. Failure to abide by the FEC's rules could subject both the party and the candidate to prosecution.

The limitations placed on *coordinated* expenditures by parties have been challenged in the Supreme Court and found acceptable. In a 2001 case, the Court was asked whether the First Amendment—which in *Colorado Republican I* had been found to permit parties to make unlimited independent expenditures on behalf of their candidates—also invalidated limitations on a party's direct contributions and *coordinated* expenditures with respect to its candidates. The Court's answer was no, because parties might serve as a "conduit" for undue influence on candidates by party contributors, even though the same contributors were free to make unlimited "independent" expenditures on behalf of candidates.[55] The Court has frequently lauded the vital role played by political parties in our political life, and has recognized the importance of strengthening the structure and policy focus of parties, but in this case, a strained five to four ruling that has become known as *Colorado Republican II*, the Court saw some possibility that corruption or the appearance of corruption could be transmitted through the party to its candidates. As a result, without legislation removing the restrictions, political parties remain today unable to provide substantial assistance to their own candidates, either through direct contributions or through coordinated expenditures.

Soft money and the BCRA. Because *Buckley* upheld sharp limits on contributions to candidates, and parties were unable to use campaign funds effectively to support their candidates, a great deal of attention was diverted to soft money as a means of influencing elections. Soft money—which can be contributed to political parties in unlimited amounts by corporations, labor unions, and individuals—was originally used by political parties for administrative and other party purposes such as getting out the vote. By definition, as noted above, it could not be used for express advocacy on behalf of candidates.

For the two decades that followed the adoption of the FECA Amendments and their treatment in *Buckley*, political parties and independent groups used soft money extensively, but in a limited way, largely for activities that paralleled campaigning.[56] However, after it was discovered that soft money could be used in so-called issue ads to criticize candidates without expressly advocating their defeat, the use of soft money by parties and independent groups became another threat to incumbents. It was incumbents, after all—on record as supporting or opposing various proposals—who were vulnerable to criticism by issue ads. As a result, soft money became a target of incumbents, and in the BCRA political parties were ultimately forbidden to accept soft money.

It would not take a campaign finance lawyer very long to figure out that the Court's establishment of the express advocacy regulatory boundary left a huge opening for unrestricted financing of campaign activity with soft money, most of which would be detrimental to incumbents. And once again, incumbent jeopardy would ultimately prompt the enactment of the campaign finance restrictions that are the heart of the BCRA. Incumbents were outraged by the criticism reflected in many of the issue ads and were determined to suppress them.[57] In 2002, as noted above, they succeeded in enacting a provision of the BCRA that banned corporations or unions from sponsoring (and sharply regulated any person who sponsored) any "electioneering communications"—defined as any broadcast that merely *mentioned* a federal candidate within thirty days of a primary election or sixty days of a general election. Again, although the provision is facially neutral, the group that suffers most from attacks by independent groups is incumbents, since they have the voting records that form the basis for these attacks.

Placing restrictions on mentioning the name of a federal candidate within thirty or sixty days of an election is a shockingly bold effort by members of Congress to protect themselves. To the surprise of most observers, a sharply divided *McConnell* Court upheld this unprecedented restraint on criticism of politicians. The Court ruled that regardless of what they explicitly said, many of the broadcast ads—most of them aimed at incumbents—were the "functional equivalent" of express advocacy and therefore could be prohibited or regulated even though they did not contain language of express advocacy.[58] The presumption was that such communications were intended to have, and likely would have, an effect on the electoral outcomes, even if their explicit message was unrelated to the campaign. In a sharply worded dissent from this ruling, Justice Antonin Scalia made it quite clear that the purpose of the law was to undermine

> the right to criticize the government. For that is what the most offensive provisions of this legislation are all about. We are governed by Congress, and this legislation prohibits the criticism of Members of Congress by those entities most capable of giving such criticism loud voice: national political parties and corporations, both of the commercial and the not-for-profit sort. It forbids pre-election criticism of incumbents by corporations, even not-for-profit corporations, by use of their general funds; and forbids national-party use of "soft" money to fund "issue ads" that incumbents find so offensive.[59]

The incumbent victory was to be short-lived. In 2007, after a change in its membership, the Supreme Court had to decide how the ban on electioneering communications might apply to a grass-roots lobbying advertisement that mentioned the name of two incumbent senators but simply asked the public to contact them on a particular pending legislative issue of interest to the sponsoring group. Since the ad would run right before the fall 2004 elections, and since one of the senators was an incumbent candidate for reelection, the ad would violate the letter of the law, unless the First Amendment said otherwise. And that's how a five to four Supreme Court saw it. The Court decided that since the justification for the ban on electioneering communications was that they were often the functional equivalent of express advocacy, any speech which was not tantamount to express advocacy was entitled to be protected.[60] This nifty bit of legal jiu-jitsu enabled the Court to reason that since protecting political speech was so important, ads like the one mentioning the senator could be banned as the functional equivalent of express advocacy only if they were "susceptible of no reasonable interpretation other than as an appeal to vote for or against a specific candidate."[61] Since the ads were susceptible of other interpretations, they could not be banned. The Court concluded that it was important to "give the benefit of the doubt to speech, not censorship."[62]

The net effect of this ruling is that, as before the passage of the BCRA, a great deal of election speech is free from controls, regardless of the source of its funding. That is good for free speech, but it magnifies the negative impact on political parties of the continued restrictions on *their* ability to raise funds to speak on behalf of themselves or to support their candidates. Put more specifically, this case now frees up a great deal of corporate, union, and individual funding for political ads that steer clear of being the functional equivalent of express advocacy, but that will nonetheless have an impact on the political environment in which elections take place. At the same time, there is no comparable lifting of the restraints on political parties, so that they can respond to all of this newly liberated electoral speech with something other than hard money. After all, it is only political parties that are prevented from receiving soft money under the BCRA. Without a change in the law, parties will have to defend themselves and their candidates with one hand tied behind their backs.

Disclosure requirements. Another basic element of our campaign finance system, and another favorite in the incumbency arsenal, is excessive campaign finance disclosure, especially disclosure of the names, identities, addresses, and occupations of contributors to candidates and political committees. When enacted, the FECA instituted mandatory public disclosure of the identity of any person who gave more than $100 to any federal candidate or campaign. The figure is now $200, which, like the doubling of the contribution limit, is, effectively, a *lower* disclosure threshold than the $100 upheld by the Supreme Court in the *Buckley* case. In fact, it is the equivalent of around $50 in 1976 dollars, so the disclosure level has been *reduced* by 50 percent. Moreover, through the magic of the Internet, *all* such information is posted promptly, thus destroying any hope of the promised political anonymity that is supposed to accompany political support. It is tantamount to a repeal of the secret ballot for anyone who gives a reportable amount to a federal candidate.

This stringent disclosure regime favors incumbents in two ways. First, people who would rather not have it known that they are opposing an incumbent, perhaps for fear of incurring his displeasure, may be deterred from contributing to a challenger.[63] Second, the extraordinary red tape that accompanies the mandated registration, reporting, and disclosure necessary to run a federal election campaign is much more expensive and time consuming for the campaign of an underfunded challenger than for an experienced incumbent.[64]

It seems clear that requiring disclosure for contributions in the range of $200 serves no purpose other than to harass challengers with expensive administrative burdens. What is the logic in a campaign finance regime that allows PACs—which are clearly "special interests"—to give $5,000 without stringent disclosure requirements, but that compels disclosure from individuals who can give no more than $2,300 at the current indexed level, and for contributions as little as $200 or so? Apparently a $5,000 contribution from a PAC is not deemed to create undue influence, so why should a $2,300 contribution from an individual? Over against the remote possibility of influence from a $2,300 contribution is the possibility that the disclosure requirement will chill individual contributions—a significant concern in our view. The same rule should apply to contributions to parties—the contributions of PACs should be disclosed, but not the permissible contributions of individuals. To be sure, contributions to parties are less likely to be chilled than contributions directly to candidates, but by the same token they are less likely to result in undue influence or corruption.

Corporations, unions, and PACs vs. political parties. Since 1907 and 1947, respectively, the federal campaign finance laws have barred corporations and unions from direct participation in federal election campaigns. Corporations and unions cannot make contributions or expenditures "in connection with" federal elections.[65] But these formal limitations have a number of statutory and constitutional exceptions.

First, internal communications—between a union and its members or between a corporation and its stockholders and administrative and executive personnel—are exempted from the ban on political activity or communication. Likewise, there is no ban on the use of corporate or union funds for voter registration and get-out-the-vote campaigns directed at the same audiences.

More significantly, corporations and unions, though barred themselves from contributing to federal candidates, may use corporate or union treasury funds to establish, administer, and solicit contributions to a PAC. Although corporations or unions cannot contribute directly from their treasuries to the funds raised by PACs, they can spend a considerable amount of money from their treasuries to run them and help them solicit contributions from their permitted donors. The PACs, in turn, can raise as much money as possible from individuals, though subject to the $5,000 limit per contributor, and then contribute that money to political candidates, though again with the $5,000 limit. Any PAC, whether or not affiliated with corporations or unions, can use contributed funds to campaign without limit for or against specific federal candidates. While all PACs must comply with strict disclosure and reporting requirements, and can raise funds only from individuals and in the limited amounts described above, at different points in time PAC money has formed a substantial amount of all federal political funding. Since incumbents have obvious influence over matters of concern to the organized groups that provide funds to PACs, incumbents tend to receive PAC financial support to a lopsided degree. Indeed, as noted above, one of the major purposes of the FECA's enactment in the 1970s was precisely to legitimize the influence of PACs, which are a very incumbent-friendly mechanism.[66]

The financial power of corporations and unions is magnified by the fact that the restrictions on their financing activities apply only to contributions to candidates or parties, expenditures for express candidate advocacy, or the sponsorship of electioneering communications close to elections. Outside these restraints, these powerful entities remain largely free to run any kind of ad mentioning, criticizing, or praising any political candidates, and to engage in any kind of election-related activity which may have an impact on the outcome of elections. So long as partisan activity does not become their primary purpose, they are free to act. In the run-up to the 2008 elections, labor unions in particular seemed to take advantage of this opportunity far more extensively than in the past.[67]

This is yet another example of the inconsistent and spotty coverage of so much of our campaign finance regulatory regime, and it has two salient consequences. First, corporate and union campaign finance power usually works to the advantage of the incumbents and the protection of the status quo, and thus to the disadvantage of challengers. Similarly, all of this largely *unregulated* campaign financing puts national political parties, which can now raise *only* hard money, at a competitive disadvantage vis-à-vis PACs, 527s (discussed below), corporations, and unions. Every time unions, corporations, or others use soft money to attack political parties and their standard-bearers, the parties' response must be financed with hard money alone. As one scholar put it, the FECA had the effect of empowering PACs and candidates over parties, and the BCRA accomplished a similar restructuring: "By encouraging the flow of money outside the party structure and into the hands of candidates and interest groups, most reform proposals unintentionally reinforced the fragmented nature of American political campaigns."[68]

527s, 501(c)s, and beyond. Further evidence of the absurd structure of the campaign finance regime—and of the second-class status of our political parties—is the dramatic increase in the use of so-called Section 527s and, more recently, Section 501(c) organizations, to serve as the recipients for corporate, union, and large individual campaign donations arguably intended, or at least likely, to affect the outcome of federal elections. These numerals do not refer to Levi's blue jeans, but to sections of the Internal Revenue Code that provide favorable tax treatment for the expenditures and receipts of non-profit organizations, including traditional charities—(c)(3), social welfare organizations—(c)(4), labor organizations—(c)(5), and trade associations—(c)(6). The code provides tax-exempt status for the receipts of such organizations and, in the case of charitable and educational groups, a tax deduction to the donor. Section 527 is of more recent origin and was created to allow organizations which are primarily political to get favorable tax treatment for their receipts. So long as they stay clear of express advocacy or coordination with candidates, and so long as partisan political activity does not become the group's major purpose, these entities get the benefit of tax exemption, without the burdens of regulation as political committees.

As soon as the Supreme Court upheld the ban on soft money contributions or expenditures by political parties, the political funding and direct political activities of 527 organizations ballooned. People and groups that could no longer give large soft money contributions to the political parties used 527s to fund their political ideas and aspirations. It is estimated that during the 2004 elections, 527s spent approximately $435 million on speech and activities designed to affect the presidential results.[69] Democratic Party groups, funded by billionaires like George Soros, set up key organizations which functioned like "shadow" political parties, running advertisements, speaking out on election issues, and organizing get-out-the-vote drives and other similar activities traditionally undertaken by parties. Indeed, one of the many rich ironies in the history of campaign finance regulation is that the BCRA was supposed to take the soft money out of federal politics, but in the first federal election after this "reform," spending by 527 groups approached the amounts spent by each of the two major parties themselves.[70] Before the 2008 elections there were reports that such groups, on both sides of the political aisle, were planning to spend up to $1 billion over the election cycle, an amount that, once again, clearly rivals the financial output of the two major political parties—even though such groups have almost none of the parties' transparency and political accountability, not to mention policy coherence. There have also been reports that established and traditional tax-favored charities are increasingly using their privileged funding status to influence public attitudes toward political issues and electoral outcomes as well.[71]

In this complex world of campaign finance rules, regulations, exceptions, and mechanisms, parties are in danger of being marginalized. Rather than playing roles at the center of our campaign finance system, with broad capacity to support their candidates and devise and present their programs, the parties have to struggle to compete with a variety of unaccountable funding sources that often operate outside the restraints with which the parties must comply.

The ban on raising or spending soft money means that all federal political party fundraising and spending must be from hard money sources. Although the hard money contribution limits are relatively generous, and are now indexed for inflation, the effect of the BCRA has been to deny the parties what had become a major source of their funding. Though the gap has been filled significantly with hard money contributions, the current law continues to reflect an unwarranted and illogical bias against political parties: parties may not raise or use soft money, while a wide variety of those who might oppose the parties' candidates or policies may do both. Thus, Section

527 groups, the exempt news media, corporations and unions eschewing express advocacy for candidates, and wealthy individuals are all privileged to use soft money to influence the electoral climate generally and specifically, while parties and their candidates can use only hard money to respond. This disparity was widely noted in the 2008 campaigns, during which groups and individuals who do not labor under the same fundraising constraints as parties spent hundreds of millions of dollars of soft money in ways that affected federal campaigns.

We have already indicated the simple solution to many of these disparities and inequities. That is to lift the restrictions on parties' coordination of their spending with their candidates. Doing so would strengthen the parties, make them more coherent in pursuing policy objectives, and counter the influence of all of the groups outside the system.

Despite the insistence of campaign finance "reformers" that all these groups should be strictly regulated, the remedy is not to suppress their activities, which include discussing issues, mobilizing voters, and energizing the electorate; these are activities that any democracy should welcome. The presence and vibrancy of these groups is an added reason to correct the comparative disadvantage of political parties, which should be the focus of political activity rather than the poor relations of the political family. Such a correction would be a welcome leveling of the political playing field. The history of campaign finance reform shows that the loopholes are found just as fast as the restrictions are imposed, and as a consequence the system is distorted and accountability dissipated. Members of Congress should recognize that the continuing effort to protect themselves against challenge is a hopeless cause, and one that has allowed a completely irrational and perverted system of campaign finance to develop. It is time to bring back political parties as the central actors of the political drama.

Public Financing of Political Campaigns

There is one other piece to our campaign finance puzzle, and that is the question of public financing of political campaigns. Not surprisingly, and despite the chronic cheerleading for more public financing of politics coming from the usual suspects, this mechanism offers up the same pattern that we have seen before: campaign finance restrictions designed to protect incumbents but masquerading as political reform.

The next chapter looks at public financing in detail. Here we make only a few large points. First, while there may be positive features to some forms of public financing of campaigns, from the very beginning public funds have come with significant strings attached—most importantly, the acceptance of "voluntary" limits on campaign spending. So, as in the case of many other so-called reforms, even the "positive" device of public funding is limits-driven and designed to *suppress*, not *expand*, political opportunities, and it too has the effect of assisting incumbents. The original presidential funding program—matching funds in the primary elections, a flat grant for the general election, and a subsidy for the conventions of the two major parties—provided a reasonable amount of money, but at the price of eliminating all private contributions in the general election. To the extent that the candidates in 2008 took federal financing for their campaigns, it was because they were confident that other independent sources would be able to pick up the slack, no matter how inefficiently. Of course the real story about public funding and the 2008 elections is that President Barack Obama became the first major-party candidate in history to reject public financing in the general election because he could raise and spend so much more through private fundraising. As a result, "Obama obliterated every political fund-raising and spending record in U.S. history."[72] He also may have obliterated public funding of presidential campaigns in the process.

Second, the real incumbency-protection mechanisms embedded in public funding can be seen in the handful of state and local public financing programs, which not only have relatively low, incumbent-protecting, competition-suppressing limits, but also contain ingenious "trigger" provisions to try to guarantee that incumbents will be able to defend themselves against a high-spending challenger. These triggers match any additional spending by an outside candidate, and do so either by giving the participating candidate more money and benefits, or by allowing the inside candidate to raise money more easily; but they always raise the spending ceilings to keep even with or surpass the spending of the outsider.[73] These schemes are designed to coerce candidates into the public funding system, with all of its limits and conditions, by making participation very attractive and by making the decision to be a "nonparticipating candidate" very unattractive, if not unavailing.

Accordingly, at bottom, these public financing schemes are just another device to protect incumbents against effective challenge. Indeed, incumbents would not pass any public funding bill without such limits and triggers. The bill currently pending in Congress, which would for the first time provide for public funding of congressional campaigns, contains such incumbent-protecting mechanisms as well.[74]

What has been tried only rarely is a system of public subsidies or campaign benefits without expenditure or other limitations on supplementary funding—in other words, a system of "floors without ceilings." Although this might be a better system for encouraging vigorous and competitive elections, the fact that it might expose incumbents to greater challenges makes its adoption unlikely.

A Better Way?

This survey of the main elements of our campaign finance system should lead the reader to several conclusions: the system is overly complex; Congress and other incumbents continue to use campaign finance "reform" to protect their own positions; and restricting political parties but not other groups—groups that were never intended to be central to a political campaign—is irrational and unfair.

So this is the system we have created, intentionally and inadvertently. Expenditures cannot be limited, which is a good thing for free speech and more-competitive elections. But contributions are limited, which greatly benefits candidates who are well-heeled or are already incumbents, and puts a premium on people and groups that can help candidates raise money more quickly (usually established interests supporting the status quo). While the Internet has emerged as a potent fundraising source for all types of federal candidates—from Barack Obama to Ron Paul—it is unlikely to be of value to congressional candidates, and recording and reporting these small contributions is an unnecessary administrative cost for campaigns that are not established. Wealthy individuals and interest groups can still support candidates of their choosing, with soft money, by avoiding express advocacy. But after the "reforms" of the BCRA, our national political parties are required to raise *all* of their funds in highly regulated ways. Thus can unaccountable individuals and interest groups play an increasingly large role in political campaigns, to the detriment of parties and, usually, challengers. The result is less electoral speech and activity directed at the broader philosophical and national interests that political parties represent, and, ironically, no significant diminution in the one thing that the campaign finance system was supposed to address—the undue influence that might foster corruption or its appearance. From the standpoint of a competitive electoral system, the BRCA has made things worse by giving significant electoral advantages to those who already hold office.

Is this truly the best we can do? Is there a better way? The next chapter will explore the alternatives.

2

Other Reforms: Would They
Make Things Better or Worse?

Critics of the current campaign finance system generally fall into three camps: those who favor more extensive regulation of private funding; those who propose expanded and perhaps even exclusive public funding; and those who advocate extensive deregulation and argue that the First Amendment alone should govern campaign finance, reasoning that the current regulatory regime is inconsistent with constitutionally protected speech or has otherwise failed to achieve its claimed objectives. Our approach falls into none of these camps; it proceeds from the assumption that the contribution limits in current law will remain, but it avoids or eliminates the adverse effects of these limits by freeing the political parties to become the principal financing sources for their candidates. The advantages to our approach—the improvements in our political process that would flow from freeing the political parties—are described in chapter 3. In this chapter we make clear why other reforms are not worth pursuing.

A recent online symposium carried the following ominous title: "Has the American Campaign Finance System Collapsed?"[1] The title does not seem too wide of the mark. It is surely extraordinary that after all the years that courts, legislatures, politicians, think tanks, and academics have been addressing the issue of campaign finance, we have arrived at such a place. At the same time, it is remarkable that so much effort should be poured into restricting the means by which citizens in a democracy are informed or inform others about their government and the doings of their representatives. The Constitution, of course, declares that "Congress shall make no law . . . abridging the freedom of speech," and the Supreme Court labors over whether this means that laws criminalizing pornography are constitutional; but the members of

Congress are permitted, without serious outcry from large portions of the public or press, to make laws that protect their own positions by restricting the amount of funding available to their challengers and the amount of information available to voters. If the First Amendment has only one purpose, surely it is to protect the right of the public to have the greatest possible influence on the electoral process. But somehow, things have gotten twisted around, so that sensible people spend their time trying to help Congress impose restrictions on political speech.

The central reason for this outcome is a focus on the wrong issue. Our current system of campaign finance regulation aims at reducing or eliminating the influence of private interests in elections by reducing the amount of money that flows into political campaigns. However, in a democratic system, the focus should be on encouraging *competitive* elections, with the elimination of money influence an important but secondary consideration. This is especially true given that years of scholarly inquiry into the relationship between campaign contributions and voting have not been able to show that lawmakers are being corrupted or subjected to undue influence. Despite the media's insistent and self-interested view that elected officials favor the interests of their contributors, academic studies have repeatedly shown that money follows policy and not the other way around.[2] One of the objectives of this book is to refocus the issue of campaign finance reform on the question of increasing the competitiveness of elections, particularly by reducing the advantages of incumbency.

As outlined in the last chapter, much legislation has failed to pass successfully through the Supreme Court's First Amendment sieve, but there has been enough so that our current campaign finance system is a mixed and incoherent hodgepodge of restrictions and exemptions. Contributions can be limited, but expenditures cannot—especially when they are made by individuals and groups acting completely independently of candidates and political parties. Candidates can contribute as much as they want to their own campaigns, but the political parties that nominated them are severely limited in what they can either contribute or expend on behalf of their candidates. Candidates and parties live with extensive controls, as do some independent groups, while other powerful actors are completely immune from regulation. In the discussion that follows, we show why the usual approaches to reform cannot by themselves be expected to lead us out of this wilderness.

More of the Same—The Internal Revenue Code (IRC) Model

In the last chapter, we discussed the development of the complex regulatory regime that now governs federal campaign finance. As originally conceived, the FECA structure was intended to be a comprehensive system of campaign finance regulation. Supreme Court decisions eliminated key elements, and cut much—but not all—of the incumbent-protective heart out of the original law. Amendments in 1976 and especially the BCRA in 2002 sought to recapture some of the ground that had been lost to the Supreme Court's application of the First Amendment.

As we have shown, additional legislation gave rise to new methods of avoidance, which in turn gave rise to new calls for additional legislation or regulation. In the sense that it attempts to close off avenues of circumvention as they become apparent, the current system resembles the Internal Revenue Code (IRC). And just as in that complex set of laws, each new restriction seems to provide a road map for subsequent avoidance. We showed in the last chapter how, almost immediately after the BCRA sought to eliminate soft money, 527 organizations suddenly appeared as yet another way for soft money to have an impact on election outcomes. Ironically, 527 organizations, like complex tax loopholes, became the new safe harbors for hundreds of millions of dollars—in this case, the soft money that could no longer go to or be used by political parties. The net effect of the new law, then, was to drive a substantial portion of campaign finance underground, and to encourage the kind of "covert speech funded by unlimited soft money" that one Supreme Court Justice has sharply criticized.[3]

Soon, there were proposals for new legislation or regulations to expand the reach of the campaign finance laws so that they also controlled Section 527 organizations and others entities (such as 501(c)(3) and (c)(4) organizations) also authorized under the IRC.[4] These proposals have not yet resulted in either new legislation or regulation of 527 groups, but the FEC has opted for ad hoc case-by-case enforcement of the rules for determining whether a group's activities render it a "political committee" subject to all of the contribution restrictions and other regulations required by FECA. As a result of that approach, the FEC imposed monetary penalties against a number of 527 groups active in the 2004 presidential campaigns, although the penalties, ranging up to $750,000, were often a very small percentage of the amounts raised and spent allegedly in contravention of FECA.[5] Next up may be an effort to treat groups of individuals as regulated political committees, another expansion of the law's coverage that has already been approved by a federal district court.[6] What this shows is that while the Congress has yet to step back into the fray, the effort to expand the scope of regulation and close off "loopholes" grinds on.

Like all regulation, the regulation of campaign finance entails the restriction of practices that, while not illegal in themselves, may be employed to circumvent the rules or the principles on which the regulatory system is based. Thus, restrictions on "bundling" of contributions—that is, one person's gathering the contributions of many others for donation to a candidate—are said to be necessary to prevent circumvention of the restrictions on individual or PAC contributions. So as individuals and groups increase the political use of Section 527 organizations, as well as Section 501(c)(3) charitable groups and Section 501(c)(4) nonprofit groups, the cry goes up that these are "loopholes" that need to be "closed" in order to prevent "evasion" of contribution restrictions. But imagination is often one step ahead of "reform." In 2008, for example, top Democratic Party operatives aligned with Senator Clinton created a for-profit campaign services organization apparently designed to allow large individual and corporate donors to "invest" without regulation—one might say launder—funds that would be used to help the Democratic presidential nominee and other Democratic candidates.[7]

In all these cases, additional regulation is proposed in order to close off the persistent efforts of voters to have something to say about who is elected. The resourcefulness of these individuals and groups suggests the importance that many attach to the expression of their views in the context of an election. For this reason, the more that Congress and the FEC try to close off financial access to the political process, the more "loopholes" will be discovered, and the more those who believe that regulation is the answer will urge regulation. More than anything else, this process seems to show the identity between money and speech itself; in a democracy, people insist on participating, and one of the most effective ways to do so is through contributing to the dissemination of ideas and the support of candidates.

What seems clear at this point is that the process of adopting new legislation and additional regulation in order to close off what are regarded as "loopholes" in the current system is a fool's errand, and for three reasons. First, as we have seen, the desire to participate in the political process through financial support of a candidate is simply too great to be restrained by laws and regulations, especially when the restraints must always comply with the requirements of the Constitution, and particularly the First Amendment. Second, the whole clanking apparatus has been set in motion to deal with a problem—corruption and undue influence associated with campaign contributions—that may not exist; certainly academic studies have been unable to draw any firm conclusion that campaign contributions substantially affect voting by lawmakers on legislation. And it is a fool's errand finally because it perpetuates a regulatory regime that has the wrong goal, one directed at preventing corruption or the appearance of corruption when it should be directed at assuring a competitive electoral process. Persistent exponents of campaign finance reform, in our view, would be wise to abandon this hopeless effort—an effort that is inconsistent not only with the First Amendment but with democracy itself—and adopt a new approach.

The Government Financing Model

Almost all government campaign-financing models proceed from a weak, and perhaps disingenuous, assumption—that by giving incumbents and challengers equal amounts of money the playing field has been leveled. In reality, incumbents start every campaign with significant advantages, and the only real chance that challengers have to overcome these advantages is to spend *more* than the incumbent they are challenging. Accordingly, if we want a competitive electoral system, we should be looking for a campaign finance regime that would allow challengers to attract more funds than incumbents. That does not mean that challengers should be given more funds or be less restricted in fundraising than incumbents, but only that the campaign finance regime should not place obstacles—as the current system does—in the paths of challengers. As the following discussion shows, the government-funded campaign finance regimes that exist today—at any level of government—are those that attempt to level the playing field by giving equal funding to both incumbents and challengers. This should come as no surprise, since it is incumbents who authorize such schemes.

"Public" or government funding of political campaigns can take many forms. In one sense, of course, our current system, which involves literally millions of Americans in making voluntary contributions to the political candidates and parties of their choice, is a truly "public" financing system, financed as it is by countless members of the public.[8] Indeed, some *laudable* forms of "public financing"—such as giving individuals a tax deduction or credit for modest political contributions—would *not* entail direct governmental involvement.

But most forms of government funding that have been enacted, whether for presidential elections or city council contests, are not of this kind. Most come with strings attached, and many come with ropes. The presidential scheme involves the government's providing matching funds in the primaries and complete funding for the general election. The string is that in order to receive the government financing candidates must agree to limit the amount they will spend on their campaigns. Many of the state and local government funding schemes have similar stipulations. As we showed in the previous chapter, spending limits—whether imposed by law or "voluntarily" agreed to as a condition of receiving the government financing—are inevitably and invariably protective of incumbents. At the presidential level, this effect may be weaker, given the national visibility and importance of presidential campaigns, and as a result challengers have beaten incumbents in three of the six pertinent presidential elections since 1976. But that percentage is never replicated or even approached in government-funded elections at the state and local levels. Indeed, in New York City, which has had one of the longest-running and most lavish government funding programs for municipal elections, the board that administers the program and dispenses the money complained recently that in the 2005 elections, with forty-four incumbents running for fifty-one council seats, "the up-hill battle for challengers proved virtually insurmountable." They concluded that "competition remains low or nonexistent in most races in which an incumbent seeks re-election." Little wonder that all but one incumbent won reelection that year.[9]

Moreover, increasingly, many of these state and local government financing schemes are designed to coerce candidates into accepting the government funding, and the severely restrictive limits that go with it, by making it burdensome to raise money privately. This is done, for example, by dramatically lowering contribution caps, and by providing additional benefits and funding to "participating" candidates to counter any expenditures made by, or even independently on behalf of, "nonparticipating" candidates.[10] Some current proposals would employ similar devices in attempting to make government financing available in congressional races.[11]

Finally, there have been proposals that would outlaw most current forms of private financing of political campaigns and replace them with a system of vouchers, coupons, or stipends that only registered voters could get, in equal amounts; these would be the only source of financial support that could be used by candidates or parties.[12] Similar proposals would mandate government financing of all elections, with no private funding of any kind permitted. The enormous problem of exempting the press from these restraints would be addressed by doctrines arguing that the press is special and constitutionally entitled to a broader right to speak than other participants in the political process.[13] But these draconian schemes, which would clearly require amending the Constitution, run afoul of the same principles and practicalities that condemn direct limits on expenditures; in the end, they restrain the speech of some participants in the process, while relatively enhancing the speech of those who are not subject to controls, especially the institutional media. All of these proposals will fail for the same reason that central economic planning fails: in a democracy, where the government's policies can be controlled by the votes of the population, there is simply too much at stake to try to ration people's influence on the outcome of elections.

Government Financing in Theory

Still, of the various reforms under consideration, public financing of election campaigns has received the most attention. As we will see, public financing in theory and public financing in fact are two different things. Although President Obama's spurning of the public financing system for presidential campaigns has dealt public financing a serious blow, the idea still commands support among those who believe—despite the evidence—that contributions to the campaigns of elected officials are something close to bribery. In addition, at the state and local level, where public funding of elections has been adopted more extensively, there are constant calls to expand and extend the public funding model. Indeed, perhaps the favorite litany of editorial board writers, second only to complaining of the corruption wrought by private financing of politics, is the call to reform politics by adopting public financing of those elections.

For incumbents, the government already finances campaigns in this respect: it makes available to officeholders all of the resources, powers, and tangible perquisites of incumbency, which they are free to use in furthering their reelection prospects. While such resources are necessary to facilitate governance, their simultaneous use to benefit the political fortunes of incumbents is inherent in the system. This is an exceedingly important fact if one assumes that the most important objective of a campaign finance regulatory regime is to promote competitive elections. Eliminating the appearance of corruption is a laudable objective, but not if it interferes with electoral competition. For the remainder of this chapter, then, we will focus on this key question—whether a particular system of campaign finance regulation promotes or suppresses electoral competition.

The various forms of government or public financing that we consider below are designed to serve a variety of purposes and to achieve a number of goals, such as relieving most lawmakers and candidates of the need to spend their time soliciting campaign contributions, reducing the significance of large contributions, and providing the resources to communicate to the public. As one of the authors of this book has written:

> Public financing can take many forms: direct grants of funds to candidates; matching funds to supplement private contributions; provisions of a variety of benefits candidates can use for their campaigns, including free mailing privileges during an election season, free radio or television time, government vouchers to purchase radio or television time, and tax credits or deductions.[14]

However, while government financing could achieve worthwhile goals, it does not often do so. It will come as no surprise to anyone who has read this far that where government funding of campaigns has actually been implemented it has tended to incorporate features that enhance the advantages of incumbency. For this reason, we will first discuss what a government financing system could achieve in theory, and then what these systems have looked like when they are actually put into effect. Indeed, the strongest argument against a government financing system is that it will inevitably be perverted by incumbents to serve their purposes rather than provide the level playing field for electoral competition.

The worthwhile things that public financing could in theory accomplish *depend on the form it takes*. For example, providing tax credits or deductions for modest or small contributions to candidates or parties could accomplish a number of objectives:[15]

1. *Provide funding for electoral communication.* Obviously, a central goal of any program of public financing of campaigns is to facilitate and support campaign communications so that candidates and parties can get their messages out to the voters. Communication with voters is the linchpin of our democratic system. Under a system based on tax credits or deductions, individuals, not the government, would determine the level and allocation of support, and all candidates and parties could expect to receive at least some measure of support. More popular ideas and candidates would get more support, but less well-known viewpoints would have an equal entitlement to subsidy, a feature missing from most of our current schemes. The amount of government involvement and potentially dangerous discretion over funding would be kept to a minimum. In many ways, this would be the most democratic form of public financing.

2. *Make elections more competitive.* Anything that makes it easier for challengers to raise funds will contribute to competitive elections. A system of contributions by individual voters—assisted and encouraged by tax benefits—will make it more likely that candidates who generate voter enthusiasm will do better at fundraising than well-known incumbents who are inattentive to their constituencies. The ability of candidates like Senator Obama and Congressman Ron Paul to raise unprecedented tens of millions of dollars in small donations on the Internet is dramatic proof of how effective a small-contribution approach can be; with the inducement of a tax credit or deduction for those small contributions, the amounts raised could have been even larger.

And this approach does not place limits on the candidates' spending or require an entire bureaucratic apparatus to dispense the funds.

3. *Reduce the appearance of corruption.* This is another strong feature of a tax-based system. The more small contributions are encouraged, the less candidates have to rely on large individual or interest group contributions that raise concerns about potential for corruption, appearance of corruption, or undue influence. The more sources of support a politician has, the less dependent he or she is on any one of them. A tax-based system of financing would give candidates a popular buffer against the charges that come with heavy reliance on interested sources of support.

4. *Ease the burdens of fundraising.* Obviously, a system that relies on private contributions, even with the sparkplug, multiplier effect supplied by tax subsidy, will not release candidates from the burdens of fundraising, as would a system of total government financing. But a tax-based financing system should ease the burden by encouraging political contributions from a much broader base.

5. *Increase political participation.* A tax-based program offers every citizen who pays income taxes, regardless of income level, a powerful incentive to support a candidate or party financially, thus increasing political participation and giving more voters a substantive stake in the outcome of an election.[16]

6. *Ease administration.* A tax-based financing system is probably the easiest of all forms of public financial support to administer, since the government is completely cut out of the process of authorizing, dispensing, or scrutinizing the use of the funds.

We note finally that a tax-based program implemented in combination with the core reforms that this book advocates—i.e., allowing political parties a greater and less fettered role in financing politics—would offer the dual benefits of expanding funding and citizen participation even more broadly.

Other forms of public support for candidates might hold promise as well. For example, a "seed money" approach, where government provides a substantial direct grant to all ballot-qualified candidates or those who could demonstrate significant voter support, has been proposed, and has even been adopted in some states.[17] This is a "floors without ceilings" mechanism, which gives qualified candidates a grubstake to launch their campaigns, but does not impose any restrictions on how much the campaign can raise and spend. This program has the advantage of greatly reducing bureaucratic supervision because there are no limits to monitor, and the agency's discretion is only a danger at the eligibility determination stage. In addition, because there are no spending limits attached to the receipt and use of the public funds, the system does not lend itself to use as an incumbent-protection device. Because of the inherent advantages of incumbency, it might make sense to provide this kind of financing only to challengers.

A program like this would level the playing field by leveling speech up, not down—in other words, it would provide a platform to support speech for all candidates, not a ceiling to restrict it. This program, like the tax-based program described above, would also nicely complement or supplement a party-centered system, since candidates in a party primary could be made eligible for grubstake funding, with the party then able to provide additional support for the general election. It is interesting that this option has not received widespread public attention and support since it was first put forward by a prominent scholar two decades ago, considering the fact that, as of the early 1990s, several states had public financing systems that made disbursements to political parties, either at the direction of taxpayers or using some predetermined formula.[18] In fact, at the presidential level, there is automatic public funding, to the tune of $16.36 million, for the nominating conventions of the two major parties (in addition to the millions that parties and host cities are permitted to raise from high rollers to underwrite the costs of hosting the conventions, undermining the notion that public funding means no private benefit).[19]

So public financing through parties is a well-established idea. The danger here, of course, is the possibility that financing to parties will freeze into place the status quo, and suppress the development of the third-party movements that have brought attention to the need for change in important areas. The presidential public financing system was condemned by one Supreme Court justice because it "enshrined the Republican and Democratic parties in a permanently preferred position."[20] Like candidates, parties should be required to compete for success and survival.

Of course, there are pitfalls that must be avoided so that government financing does not perpetuate some of the ills of the current system. For example, since public financing systems are usually designed by incumbents, they frequently contain elements that disadvantage challengers. Incumbents almost always want to put spending limits in a government financing program as the condition for receiving any of its benefits. Superficially, this seems fair, but when one considers the advantages in publicity and name recognition that incumbents enjoy, it becomes clear that expenditure limitations are favorable to the reelection of those who already hold office. Nevertheless, the Supreme Court has upheld as constitutional a "voluntary" program in which a challenger gives up the right to raise additional funds, and incumbents ever since have been happy to put this provision into government financing programs to make sure that challengers will not be able to outspend them. Another favorite of incumbents is the lifting of expenditure limits on a participating candidate (most often an incumbent) if a well-funded candidate (most often a challenger) or independent group (most often anti-incumbent) shows up on the scene. These devices, designed to scare off or deter serious challengers and to counter the speech of critical independent groups, make most current forms of public financing thinly veiled incumbent-protection devices.

Regrettably, even those few public financing programs that were not voted into place by incumbents—that were instead the product of popular referendums championed by campaign-reform groups—typically have severe limits and restrictions on contributions and expenditures as well. This is because the mission of these groups is not primarily to increase electoral competition, but to take as much private money out of the political process as possible on the premise that better campaigns and government will result. As a consequence, government becomes less responsive to the voters and the essence of democracy is compromised. Accordingly, as we discuss below, whether a government financing system improves the quality of government or simply perpetuates existing imbalances depends critically on what kind of public financing devices are employed.

Government Financing in Practice

In practice, public financing regimes that actually advance the cause of competitive elections are the exception. Most are matching-funds regimes, where candidates raise money privately but receive a matching amount from the relevant government, supplying a kind of multiplier effect to their private fundraising. That is how the presidential primary public financing system is structured, and how some of the proposed legislation for public funding of congressional campaigns would work. The match is usually dollar-for-dollar for contributions up to $250, although some programs, like New York City's, are much more lavish, and match that modest contribution four-, five-, or sixfold. All of these programs involve a great deal of government bureaucracy, red tape, and the potential for political favoritism and discrimination, and almost all favor incumbents by imposing "voluntary" spending limits as the condition for receiving the benefits.

Flawed laws. In the real world, it turns out that incumbents will not enact public funding programs unless they contain various limitations that protect them against a well-funded challenger. The most popular form of incumbent protection is to require a challenger who accepts government funding to limit expenditures to a predetermined ceiling. In this case, the incumbent cannot be outspent and can reap all the real benefits of incumbency. If, on the other hand, the challenger prefers to be privately funded, the laws increasingly have been designed to relieve the participating candidate (usually the incumbent) from limits and restrictions when a nonparticipating candidate reaches a certain level of expenditures or commits to using a certain amount of personal funding. The incumbent is then able to use the advantages of incumbency to raise campaign funds in an amount that equals or exceeds the funds available to the challenger. Thus, through trigger mechanisms that penalize a nonparticipating candidate and provide "rescue funds" to the participating candidate, the system exerts heavy pressures on all candidates to accept public financing and the expenditure limits that favor incumbents.[21] These second-generation public financing models, carefully designed to protect incumbents and penalize those who are "nonparticipating," go well beyond the model that started the ball rolling: the public financing of presidential elections.

Presidential public financing. The presidential public financing system is relatively simple: it provides matching funds for primary elections and full funding for general elections. Candidates who accept public funding must agree not to exceed various state-by-state ceilings on expenditures during the primary period, an overall national spending ceiling in the primaries, and a nationwide spending ceiling in the general fall election.[22]

Although the Supreme Court has upheld the presidential public financing system against constitutional challenge as serving a number of positive purposes, it still presents several potential problems. First, in restricting spending by the presidential candidates, the expenditure limitations themselves encourage partisans of each candidate—who are, quite legitimately in a democracy, eager to influence the outcome of the election—to spend money independently and set up and fund groups that will do the same. These individuals and groups, as we have indicated, do not have the same accountability as candidates and parties and, depending on how they conduct their campaigns, are not subject to the contribution limits that candidates and parties face. So, although the public financing system eliminates private money from the formal campaigns of the presidential candidates, it also limits accountability by reducing the information the public receives about who is actually helping a presidential candidate.[23] Second, the very structure of the presidential public funding scheme may tend to favor one kind of candidate over another. The dean of campaign finance scholars, Herbert Alexander, maintained that the major changes in the campaign finance system after Watergate, such as limits on contributions and public funding of presidential races, helped Jimmy Carter win the presidency over candidates like Senator Henry M. Jackson and Congressman Morris K. Udall, who would most likely have raised considerably more money under the old system from larger contributors without public funding.[24]

Similarly, scholar John Samples has observed that state-by-state limits on media spending during primary elections, in addition to the overall national spending limits, were designed to thwart candidacies like those of Senator Eugene McCarthy and Governor George Wallace, who had strong geographic pockets of ideological or regional support and needed to make themselves better known elsewhere.[25] The courts have also recognized that the public funding of the general election denies average citizens the right to provide tangible support to the candidate of their choice and thus to help that candidate get the would-be donor's message out to the public.[26] But court recognition of this right has not resulted in the invalidation of the presidential public funding system.

The funding for the presidential system uses a tax check-off device, which allows taxpayers to designate a nominal amount from their federal income tax payment to go to the presidential election fund. It is not a direct government appropriation, so there is an element of taxpayer choice involved in the level of financing. In this respect, the check-off, as it is called, has become something of a barometer of public support for the public financing system, since contributions to the fund are voluntary and do not entail any increase in the taxpayer's total payment. By this measure, the public funding program has suffered a dramatic decline in public support over the years, dwindling from a high of 28.6 percent in 1977 to a current low of approximately 9.1 percent. The initial check-off amount was $1 per taxpayer, but at that level the fund was not able to collect sufficient resources. So in 1993 the check-off amount was raised to $3 per taxpayer. Now some public financing advocates are proposing that the check-off amount be raised to $6 per taxpayer to insure that the fund has ample resources.[27] The falloff in public support should not be surprising; the taxpayer is not able to direct the funds to the candidate or party of his or her choice, as would be the case with a tax-credit or tax-deduction program, and supporting a public financing scheme—even at no direct cost to the taxpayer—is apparently not seen as worthwhile. Given its declining popularity and its adverse effects, the system of public funding for presidential elections should be abandoned and replaced by a straightforward system of political party funding.

Not willing to take a chance on the continued fickleness of the public, many of the newer public financing programs would pay for the campaigns out of general treasury funds appropriated by the legislature, not out of check-offs approved by taxpayers. In effect, then, the incumbents would now be in charge of providing, at taxpayer expense, the public financing of their own reelection campaigns. In New York City, for example, the City Council continues to raise what is called "the match." It started out as a 1 to1 (dollar-for-dollar) match, up to the first $1,000 of a qualifying contribution. Since then the match has gone up to 6 to 1 (every dollar contributed is matched by six from the city), but the amount matched has gone down to $175, for a total match of $1,050 per qualified contributor. The amount of money matched per contributor has not been significantly increased, but less affluent contributors can more effectively subsidize their chosen candidate, and presumably more of them can participate. Yet this effort to give participants more public bang for the privately raised buck has nevertheless not put a dent in the incumbent reelection rates. The New York City experience shows that with the ever-present insistence on spending ceilings as the price for receiving public funds, challengers can rarely overcome the built-in advantages of incumbents. As we observed above, in 2005, only one City Council incumbent failed to win reelection in New York City, and all received matching funds.

State and local programs. Public financing at state and local levels is more widespread than one would expect. Depending on which study one consults, there are public financing programs in one form or another in sixteen to twenty-five states.[28] The mechanisms take three forms. Some involve matching funds, like the presidential primary system; in these cases, the match is usually dollar for dollar for small contributions, but some jurisdictions, like New York City, offer a more generous match. A second form, mostly involving the older systems, offers flat grants of a fixed amount for those candidates, and sometimes even those political parties, that have reached a certain level of viability and establishment. The third form, a newer form, is the so-called Clean Election model, which involves almost total government funding of campaigns for those candidates who raise a certain amount of money in very small increments, typically $5 each from a large number of contributors. Once that test has been passed, the candidate is eligible for full government funding of the campaign.

Almost all the public financing programs have spending limits which participants must adhere to. The more recently enacted and proposed systems—following the Millionaire Amendment format adopted in the BCRA—contain various triggering mechanisms that give participating candidates (read: incumbents) more government money or more private fundraising rights if a nonparticipating candidate approaches or exceeds the spending limits. In many places, public money or increased fundraising rights are given to participating candidates to counter speech by outside groups and individuals who either oppose participating candidates or support nonparticipating candidates. As one campaign attorney put it: "Every time you raise a buck for yourself, you raise a buck for your opponent."[29] Thus, the ceiling is continually raised for participating candidates, to enable them to counter the speech of nonparticipating candidates. Though these two categories are not automatically synonymous with incumbents and challengers, it is unlikely that an incumbent will have to raise or spend private funds where government funding is available unless his or her challenger has personal resources or significant private financial backing. It remains in the general interest of incumbents to force challengers into a system of spending limits, by attempting to neutralize any benefits that flow to those who do not participate in the public financing scheme. And the mechanism in almost all of the public financing schemes is limitations on expenditures, one of the most powerful pro-incumbent devices.

The two most well-known Clean Election public financing programs are in Arizona and Maine.[30] Long heralded as good government models by the foundation-funded reform groups that lobby for those programs, they very much resemble some of the most prominent bills pending in Congress: after raising a qualifying amount of money in very small increments, funded candidates are given flat grants for their campaigns, supplemented by additional grants to counter spending by nonparticipating opponents or independent speech benefiting those opponents. Candidates who participate can spend no more than the government gives them, but, of course, those amounts will be increased to counter speech that is not publicly financed.

Although assessment of the results tends to be made through a highly partisan lens, even the Government Accountability Office report failed to find significant and unqualified accomplishments from either system in terms of electoral reform or citizen satisfaction. Some have suggested that in Maine, the system tended to entrench incumbents even more,[31] while in Arizona, the public funding system appears to have been manipulated by an incumbent Democratic governor to defeat a privately financed Republican opponent.[32] Public financing schemes in other states and localities have likewise received, at best, mixed reviews. And in some of those states, where check-off mechanisms or other means of registering voter or taxpayer support are used, there has been a decline in support just as there has been for the federal presidential system.[33] Finally, and perhaps most telling, some states have even started to roll back and repeal previously established public financing programs because of citizen disinterest and lack of support.[34] Despite a well-financed reform effort in California in 2006, voters decisively rejected a statewide ballot initiative for public financing of state elections.

After this review, it is difficult to disagree with the following summary by Stephen Hoersting, testifying before the Senate Committee on Rules and

Administration in 2007: "Taxpayer financing of election campaigns does not improve citizens' perceptions of government; does not increase the competitiveness of elections; does not lead to more political participation by citizens; does not lead to better representation in our statehouses and would not lead to better representation in Congress, if adopted. Taxpayer financing is expensive, places non-participants at an unfair disadvantage, and, as the polls show, is not what the People want from their government or candidates."[35]

Federal Proposals for Public Funding

At the federal level, bills providing for public funding of congressional campaigns have passed the House or the Senate or both on a number of occasions and have taken various forms—almost all of which, again, have involved the imposition of spending limits as a condition of receiving the public funds and/or benefits. Currently there are several bills pending in Congress which in the aggregate constitute a grab bag of all of the various public financing proposals and programs of the last several years.

Senate Bill 1285 is typical of the current crop, and follows the usual pattern of favoring incumbents. It attempts to discourage private fundraising by allowing the publicly financed candidate to match the funds obtained by the candidate who is privately financed. Once again, this is a system that looks fair, since it applies to all candidates, including incumbents. But in reality S. 1285 is highly favorable to incumbents, who already have name recognition and have been able to use public resources while in office to inform voters about their achievements. The bill's attempt to protect incumbents is so transparent that it seems to reflect a belief in both the naiveté of the voters and the likely acquiescence of the media, which—because incumbents make sure that the campaign finance laws exempt the media from their restrictions and controls—are also beneficiaries of a system in which privately financed speech is limited. The media support campaign finance restrictions; the incumbents exempt the media from those restrictions. You do the math.

To be eligible for taxpayer financing under S. 1285, a candidate must raise a number of $5 "qualifying contributions" from registered voters in his or her own state or district. At the outset of the campaign, each tax-funded candidate is allowed to raise a modest amount of seed money from private sources (donations of up to $100 per individual are permitted) to assist in rais-ing the necessary qualifying contributions. In return, the candidate receives a fixed sum of taxpayer money and agrees not to raise any private money during the primary or general election campaigns. If a tax-funded candidate is being outspent by a privately funded candidate, the act provides a mechanism—called "matching funds" or "fair fight funds" in S. 1285—for the participating candidate to stay financially competitive with the opposing nonparticipating candidate.[36] Not only would participating candidates (read, again, incum-bents) receive government funds to match the private spending of any non-participating candidate, but they would also receive funds to counter any money spent by independent groups or individuals *either* opposing the par-ticipating candidate or supporting the nonparticipating opponent. This is one of the particularly pernicious features of the more recent public financing schemes, since it not only discourages candidates from operating outside the public financing scheme, but is also intended to neutralize the impact even of independent political speech by providing government funds to counter it.

Most of the bills pending in Congress, of which S. 1285 is the most well known, contemplate that candidates could opt for traditional private financ-ing, despite all of the relative disadvantages the bills would impose by bene-fiting and subsidizing the participating candidates. But one of the pending bills would also attempt to make public financing of House campaigns *mandatory* in the general election, a move which would appear to be flatly and unarguably unconstitutional.[37]

What would the enactment of such a "clean money" bill accomplish? It would certainly not reduce the role of private financing in federal campaigns. In our major national experiment with clean-money financing of federal elections—the full public funding of general election campaigns by at least Democratic and Republican presidential nominees throughout the 1990s—there was robust growth of the soft money system used by the national and local political parties to support their candidates. When that was eliminated by the BCRA in 2002, it was immediately supplanted during the 2004 presidential campaign by so-called 527 groups, which spent upwards of $500 million to influence the outcome of the elections. This was a net loss for the cause of reform, because the activities of these groups were carried on with much less of the disclosure and accountability that at least accompanied the national parties' use of soft money. In the 2008 presidential election, 527s continued to be extremely active but were joined by nonprofit and charitable organizations in election-related spending reminiscent of the soft money spending by parties, unions, and interest groups in previous elections. Their spending was estimated at $435 million. Here again there was less accountability because of the confidentiality that is permitted by our tax laws.

The lesson that should be taken from all of this is that presidential elections—and in reality all federal elections—are too important to be straitjacketed within spending restraints. Congress may want to limit the funding of challengers through a variety of devices, but the desire of voters to participate in the American democracy—for ideological as well as self-interested reasons—will not be cabined. The larger and more important the government becomes in the lives of the American people, the higher will be the stakes for those wishing to influence who wields the government's powers.

In addition to all of the triggers that require giving more money and benefits to participating candidates, the level of bureaucracy required to administer this complex program is staggering. Not only will the government have to determine how much the nonparticipating candidate has been spending (to determine when to give the participating candidate more offsetting funds and benefits), but there will be the additional difficulty of determining whether speech is "against" the participating candidate or "in favor of" the nonparticipating candidate. When campaign controls on independent speech "for" or "against" candidates were first proposed, one wag asked how the government would assess a campaign button that read "Reluctantly for Humphrey." The effort to determine whether independent speech is "matchable"—which will involve difficult decisions about how to interpret the First Amendment—will be occurring in the heat and hectic pace of the last weeks of a campaign, with every bureaucratic decision determining whether a participating candidate will be getting more money to use before election day. (This is not to mention the post-election litigation we can anticipate from a losing participating candidate, who will demand a new election because he was improperly denied the "fair fight" funds to which he was entitled.)

With voter participation in public financing declining, with some of the most widely heralded plans receiving at best mixed reviews, and with the presidential public funding system apparently in meltdown, it seems surprising that reformers are mounting an even more insistent campaign for public financing of congressional elections. The reason for this is ultimately a misplaced belief in the power of campaign finance to influence lawmakers, and a failure to recognize the role of existing public finance laws in assisting incumbents. In 2006, the New York City Campaign Finance Board urged more public funding for the New York City system, noting regretfully that "the strongest predictor of electoral success is incumbency."[38] This is perhaps the most telling critique of public funding proposals. After twenty years of such "success," the incumbency rate has been affected, if at all, only by mandatory term limits. How's that for electoral competitiveness? And the mayor, who also cheerleads for the system, is a billionaire who casually eschewed using that system in order to spend "whatever it takes" to get elected and reelected.

But maybe it is not so surprising, since in the reformer's universe, if something does not work, then the solution must be to try more of it. That has been the pattern with regulation of private funding, and it is apparently the pattern with advocacy of public funding. It is like throwing good money after bad. This summary of the problem is offered by the Center for Competitive Politics:

> Government-financed elections are the ultimate fool's gold of campaign finance regulation. Proponents of government-financed elections promise improved perceptions of government, "better" representation of elected officials, more competitive elections, and more political participation by the public. Studies show that not only do government-financed elections not deliver the promised results but they actually decrease confidence in government, all while being a poor use of taxpayer dollars.[39]

Ultimately, the experience with government financing of political campaigns is a cautionary tale. It shows that allowing governments—i.e., incumbents—to structure campaign finance systems will almost always result in a system that benefits officeholders and weakens the essential electoral competition that is necessary in a democracy. Government financing of campaigns does not actually remove private financing from politics; it only redirects it. A recent *Wall Street Journal* editorial pointed out, for example, that even tax-exempt, deductible contributions to the Clinton Library could be a basis on which private groups could seek and gain influence over a President Hillary

Clinton.[40] If our purpose is indeed to eliminate private interests entirely from the financing of political campaigns, then public financing is indeed a fool's errand for fool's gold: private interests cannot and should not be eliminated from something as important as elections, and public financing will almost inevitably be manipulated to further entrench incumbents, rather than providing—as it should—a means to "throw the rascals out."

From the Framers—A Minimalist Approach

There is, of course, one model that has been available for quite some time and provides a strikingly different approach from the various regulatory schemes for control of spending. That model is the First Amendment's protection of freedom of speech, assembly, petition, and press. Viewed as a policy guide, the First Amendment would posit *no limits* on campaign giving or spending; the source of the contribution, the amount of the contribution, and the length and content of the message paid for by the contribution would be unregulated. It would address concerns about the influence of funding sources on elected officials as either irrelevant, as many studies have shown them to be,[41] or remedied by full and immediate disclosure of contributions large enough to be influential, with the electorate taking the information into account when it votes. Concerns about enhancing and expanding political opportunity could be addressed by providing various forms of public subsidies, but without onerous conditions and restrictions, much as public forums are provided for those who would speak or communicate. In other words, any government funding scheme would provide floors to support competitive campaigns, not expenditure ceilings to limit them.

This model rests on traditional First Amendment principles, requiring minimal government interference with speech activity and maximum opportunity for a wide variety of communications. It also is based on the premise that robust political speech is not the enemy of democracy but its engine, and that government control of free speech is antithetical to democracy. Since such controls are often evaded anyway, their effect is not to take the money out of politics but to take the First Amendment out of politics.

This deregulatory and minimalist model has one drawback, however: as a practical matter, it is probably not politically feasible. The adoption of the

BCRA and all its predecessors shows that incumbent protection is a strong impulse in Congress. It is highly unlikely that Congress would remove all limits on campaign finance, just as it is highly unlikely that Congress would adopt a public funding model that does not place an incumbent-protecting cap on expenditures. The fact that the Supreme Court has endorsed contribution limits, even if only for the limited purpose of preventing corruption or the appearance of corruption, will make the existence of such limits a sine qua non for any reform Congress is likely to adopt. As a practical matter, the campaign finance options available are limited to a continuation of the current IRS-like system or a public funding mechanism, and both have severe deficiencies if our objective is—as it should be—more competitive elections. Accordingly, we believe that removing the limits on party expenditures, while retaining some contribution limits, is likely to be the best reform that is politically achievable.

Still, there are other more exotic ideas that have been advanced in the past because of dissatisfaction with the current system. We review these and their likely effectiveness in the next section.

Other Proposals for Campaign Finance Reform

Over the years, a variety of exotic proposals for improving our campaign finance system have been advanced. Most of them have appeared in books and academic journals, though some have been the subject of legislative proposals. Virtually all are based on the false premise that private campaign financing creates undue influence over lawmakers, and they thus sacrifice electoral competitiveness in order to reduce the role of private money in politics. This approach has the effect of turning the First Amendment on its head, making it an enemy of free speech rather than its guarantor. Never mind that most academic studies have shown that money does not drive issues, but the other way around—groups and individuals contribute to candidates with whom they are already in policy agreement.

Free television time. A major reason that political campaigns need to raise so much money is the cost of broadcast advertising, especially television. Although federal law requires broadcasters to provide qualified federal candidates with reasonable access, the candidates have to pay for that time, albeit at the lowest available rates.[42] To address the issue of TV costs, there have been numerous proposals to provide candidates with free television time. In the 1990s there was a strong push on this front.[43]

Because it has superficial plausibility, free television time has been one of the favorite items in the reformers' playbook. The problem is that free TV time for politicians is anything but free. Indeed, there are five fundamental flaws with such proposals.

First, of course, the TV time is not free to the broadcasters. The proposals would, in effect, confiscate the property of broadcasters and impose a restriction on freedom of the press. While the courts have accepted some regulation of broadcast media, and have even approved requiring broadcasters to sell air time to politicians, forcing broadcasters to give that time away is a violation of basic rights of property and an abridgement of First Amendment free speech guarantees.

Second, free television time is not even free to the candidates. Most proposals require candidates to agree to spending limits or limits on use of personal funds in order to get the free time. In other words, restraints that the Supreme Court declared unconstitutional when imposed on candidates directly are again being introduced as conditions to the receipt of government-mandated, broadcaster-delivered benefits. And, once again, expenditure limits provide major advantages to incumbents, who almost always have free access to television because of their functions as officeholders. The opportunity to limit the expenditures of challengers in exchange for a limited amount of free television time is thus too good for incumbents to miss.

Third, many proposals require candidates to toe various format and content lines when they use their free time. Government is literally dictating the way candidates deliver their message. For example, in some proposals the candidate would have to appear personally in the ads, and the ads would have to be at least sixty seconds long. A few require the candidate to face the camera at all times. Once again, it would be unthinkable for government to dictate these terms and conditions directly, apart from using them as the cudgel against candidates who want the free air time. And once these limits are established as precedent, there will be plenty of opportunities for incumbents to place further restrictions on what is communicated; it's not hard to imagine restrictions, for example, on "personal attacks" within a week of the election. There are already disputes between campaigns about the fairness of campaign ads—and requests that broadcasters refuse to run them because of their supposed inaccuracy. These claims will become even more insistent and well-founded when the government is actually paying for ads.

Fourth, the proposals almost all reserve time exclusively for Democrats and Republicans, through eligibility and other formulas that effectively exclude all other candidates. The same type of exclusionary eligibility mechanism which has been used for presidential public financing would be imported into the wider area of congressional elections. Nor would free time be available to nonpartisan groups who wanted to address the same issues the politicians had discussed during their free broadcast time.

Finally, the enforcement of a free-TV-time proposal, available for all federal elections, would be an administrative nightmare, especially if the benefit were available to state and local candidates as well. But even if free time were limited solely to federal elections, how broadcasters allocated time among candidates, and balanced that against the broadcasters' need to schedule commercial advertising, would inevitably give rise to disputes and litigation.[44]

Communication vouchers. A related but less problematic approach would be for government to provide candidates with communication vouchers which they could exchange for the purchase of broadcast time or advertising space. This would differ from flat-out public funding in that it would subsidize only campaign communications. The government would make the funds available to redeem the vouchers, but by allowing the broadcasters to charge for the time, this plan avoids the gross intrusion on broadcasters that free-time proposals represent. Candidates could choose to spend the vouchers in various media, not just broadcasting. Important questions of candidate eligibility would remain. Limiting the vouchers in effect to candidates for the two major parties, as has mostly been the case with presidential public financing, affords too narrow a range of political opportunity and advocacy. On the other hand, making vouchers contingent on some significant indication that a candidacy is serious and has support would give rise to disputes.

Although no voucher system has yet been implemented, it is likely that such a system would contain the usual provisions that limit the expenditure of other campaign funds. Again, such limits-driven systems suppress political speech and activity, and will inevitably inure to the benefit of incumbents.

Patriot dollars. Two Yale Law professors, Bruce Ackerman and Ian Ayres, have proposed a system of so-called patriot dollars.[45] These would be in effect government-issued credit cards, made available to all registered voters, in equal and nominal amounts. Each voter could use that card to subsidize the candidate of his or her choice. All voters regardless of income would get the same amount, and thus, in the aggregate, lower-income people and communities would gain some significant political power. Candidates across the political spectrum could be the beneficiaries. In a way, this is very similar to the idea of a tax-based system of private financing, with tax credits or deductions for small political contributions. In this case, however, the government would be underwriting the donation directly, and the system would provide an opportunity for low-income people who do not pay taxes to provide financial support to candidates. Either way, the cost of the contribution is defrayed by the government and amounts to a transfer from the taxpayers to the voters. If every registered voter in the country were given such a $10 voucher, that would generate the same $2 billion in funding per election cycle that the current proposals for public financing of congressional elections are estimated to cost.

This system would avoid the questions associated with how to allocate television time, and would not burden any particular group in society other than the taxpayers themselves. However, it would have other drawbacks, particularly that of favoring incumbents. At the beginning of any campaign season, incumbents are ordinarily the best-known candidates, and they would be likely to scoop up most of the available patriot dollars before other candidates were in the field. Moreover, some seed money would be necessary for candidates to be able to appeal for contributions in patriot dollars, and this money would be difficult to come by until a candidate had become well-enough known to attract support. If candidates were able to raise or use private funds to appeal for patriot-dollar financing, incumbents would again be the first in the field, and if—as is likely—the proposal was implemented through a restriction on spending non-patriot dollars, that would also give incumbents an advantage. Finally, the proposal does not address the question of outside support for a candidate.

Only patriot dollars. The possibility that outside support for a candidate might distort a government financing system is addressed by a darker version of the patriot-dollar approach which has been championed by other academics. It pursues the leveling of campaign involvement to its logical extreme. Under this theory, if we believe in "one person, one vote," we must implement that principle not only at the ballot box, but at the soap box as well. Just as all citizens must have equal voting rights, all citizens must have equal political participation rights, including participation in campaign funding.

Accordingly, this approach would provide all citizens, or all registered voters, or perhaps all adults in America, with a small grant in the form of a voucher or coupon which that person could contribute to or use for political activity.[46] But that coupon or voucher would be *the only legal means* of financing political activity. People could not use their individual wealth and groups could not use their organized wealth in any fashion for political ends. The vouchers or dollars could be given to candidates, parties, or interest groups, and those groups could fund their activities out of those subsidies, but out of no other sources. In effect this is a proposal to outlaw all private funding of politics. Even the media would be subject to this regime, at least insofar as editorial endorsements of candidates are concerned, although the news functions would be exempt from the voucher/coupon system.

In the unlikely event that this proposal passed constitutional review, it would substantially reduce the level of campaign funding available to candidates, and once again provide a significant benefit to incumbents. Incumbents would get the dominant share of those funds that are made available (significant amounts would never be used), and any reduction in the total funds available for campaign expenses benefits incumbents, who are almost always better known than their challengers and need less campaign funding to introduce themselves to voters. In addition, there are countless ways in which people with resources, media access, and other levers of influence could use those capacities to influence the outcome of elections. They could work through the entertainment industry, bankroll foundations, organize lobby groups, influence public discussion, and do a myriad of things to affect the information that reaches voters and the environment in which elections occur. As Plato once said, "Let me write a nation's songs, and I care not who makes its laws."

The donation booth. Another academic proposal calls for a "donation booth."[47] Its premise is that undue influence by large contributors can be eliminated by making them anonymous. Two academics thus have argued for a cutout between the donor and the politician, so that the latter does not know who the former is. Contributions would be made anonymously to a blind trust controlled by a trustworthy company. The funds would then be turned over to a refurbished Federal Election Commission (made up of trust-worthy retired federal judges) that would disburse the funds to the recipient candidates, who in turn would not know who their donors were or how much they contributed. Various procedural safeguards are proposed to preserve the donors' anonymity and to undermine donors' ability to reveal that they have given a large gift. If in fact contributors give to those who agree with them on policy, and not for the purpose of seeking influence, this idea makes sense. Challengers and incumbents will receive anonymous funding for their campaigns, while the undue influence of money that many believe exists will be eliminated. With the right kind of cutout, donors would not have to worry about retribution for giving to a particular candidate, and the public would not have to worry about the corrupting influence of donations.

The trouble with this proposal is that most donors give only after they have been solicited in some way. If this is done through personal contact, it is difficult to see how a contribution could be anonymous. Imposing a penalty on a donor for telling a candidate of the donor's financial support—which seems to be a requirement of such a system—would be a violation of the First Amendment. Without solicitation, very little money would be likely to flow into campaigns, and that would once again be favorable to incumbents. On the other hand, if this proposal were to be implemented, political parties would be perfect in the role of a cutout—that is, as a recipient between the donor and the candidate. If the fear is that contributions to parties will stipulate their use by a particular candidate, this can be addressed without free speech implications.

Instantaneous Internet disclosure. Finally, one proposal, which is the flip side of the donation booth, would involve disclosure as a cure-all for campaign finance ills. The theory is that so long as voters had information about who was contributing how much to which candidates, they could make the proper assessment of questions of access and influence and vote accordingly. The way to facilitate that information is to make it instantly available on the Internet. Although federal campaigns now must disclose their contributors periodically, the law does not require instantaneous disclosure on the Internet. Technologically speaking there is no reason why that could not be accomplished. Instant disclosure would certainly be friendlier toward the First Amendment than sharp limits on contributions, especially if the disclosure threshold were raised considerably above its current $200 level. As we indicated above, that level is even less, adjusted for inflation, than the $100 threshold enacted in 1974; it also imposes a huge administrative and expense burden on candidates and violates the political privacy of donors— without any significant benefit in terms of public information about the sources of a candidate's support.

If enhanced disclosure were coupled with an easing of contribution restrictions to candidates, committees, and parties, there would be some beneficial consequences. If it is simply more disclosure for its own sake, then it barely addresses the more systemic problems posed by our campaign finance system. In any case, disclosure of contributions can result in retaliation by officeholders against those who are contributing to their challengers.

Conclusion

It's clear that all reform proposals have serious deficiencies. Most of them would, in practice, be favorable to incumbents because they would result in expenditure limits. The reason these proposals have any currency is that they proceed from the mistaken idea that the purpose of campaign finance restrictions is to limit the influence of campaign contributions on lawmakers. This is not a bad idea, but it is far less important than assuring a competitive electoral system. Indeed, a truly competitive electoral system provides a more efficient mechanism for disclosing corruption or undue influence than any of the regulatory and public financing ideas discussed in this chapter or in chapter 1. In a truly competitive electoral system, each party has an incentive to discover and publicize cases of alleged corruption or undue influence on the part of the other party or its candidates. The voting public can then decide whether the complaining party has made a strong case. For this approach to work, however, the underlying system itself has to be competitive, and that can occur, we believe, only if political parties are able to fund the campaigns of their candidates, particularly those of challengers.

3

The Benefits of Lifting Campaign Finance Restrictions on Parties

As we showed in chapter 1, almost every major element of "reform" legislation adopted by Congress has been intended to protect incumbents. Most of these provisions have been invalidated by the Supreme Court, but two still remain—stringent contribution limits and restrictions on the ability of political parties to finance the campaigns of their candidates. In this chapter, we will show that even if contribution limits are left in place, eliminating the restrictions on parties will create the kind of competitive electoral system that a healthy democracy requires.

The first major effort to reduce the role of the political parties in the electoral process occurred in 1940, with the adoption of the Hatch Act, which put an overall limit of $3 million on how much national party committees could raise and spend annually, and a $5,000 limit on contributions to them. This restriction, which fit well with the earlier Progressive Era efforts to restrict the role of parties, was probably the genesis of the candidate-centered campaign finance regime we have today. Thereafter, as outlined in detail in chapter 1, Congress placed limitations on what parties could contribute to their own candidates and on the expenditures that parties could make in coordination with their candidates. Although most expenditure limitations have been struck down by the Supreme Court, the restrictions on parties remain and have been upheld as constitutional.

In the BCRA, Congress again attempted to limit the ability of parties to provide assistance to their own candidates, first by requiring parties to choose between coordinated and uncoordinated spending (a restriction ultimately struck down by the Supreme Court), and then by outlawing the use by parties of the same soft money that is now freely available to all other groups—

including corporations, unions, and the infamous 527s. The odd part about this restriction on parties is not only that parties continue to be disadvantaged relative to all other players in the political system, but also that the extreme decentralization brought about by this restriction results in less disclosure of the use of soft money.

In the end, it is not difficult to understand the motive for keeping parties so severely disadvantaged: political parties are the only institutions in our society that have both a consistent interest in providing financing to challengers, and the ability to raise sufficient funds for a credible challenge to incumbents. That's why even though most other incumbent-protective elements of the campaign finance laws have been eliminated, the restrictions on parties are still important. They remain, indeed, the most important impediments to the development of a truly competitive electoral system.

In this chapter, we outline how freeing the parties from the restrictions that now exist in campaign finance laws will eliminate many of the deficiencies in our current electoral system, will improve and increase the information available to voters, and will make the candidates and the parties themselves more accountable.

A More Competitive Electoral System

Despite the Supreme Court's decision in *Buckley* to strike down expenditure limits, the remaining restrictions in the campaign finance laws have enabled incumbents to retain and benefit from most of their inherent advantages. Accordingly, in the ordinary election year, incumbents almost always win. Reelection rates for incumbents in the House of Representatives were 94 percent in 1996 and 98 percent in 1998, 2000, and 2002.[1] This does not say much good about our democracy. Members of the House are fond of referring to themselves as the people's representatives, but does anyone believe that the American people are so pleased with the operation of their government that they gladly reelect virtually every one of their representatives? Opinion polls regularly show that Congress is near the bottom of the scale among U.S. institutions in which the public has confidence. Yet a member of Congress who hasn't actually been indicted can look forward confidently to being reelected.

There is not much that can or should be done about many of the advantages of incumbents. Certain benefits—such as a government-paid staff (to do casework and respond to constituent questions), franked mail, a district or state office, and the media attention that comes with being a member of Congress—are an irreducible part of holding elective office in a democracy.[2] The fact that these elements produce substantial name recognition and other benefits simply cannot be avoided. However, because incumbents already have so many advantages over challengers, our campaign laws should rectify or compensate for this imbalance in order to assure a healthy competition for political office.

Unfortunately, however, far from correcting an imbalance, the current candidate-centered campaign finance system exacerbates it. The data show, for example, that in order to overcome the incumbent's inherent advantages a challenger must be at least as well-funded as the incumbent. As Goidel, Gross, and Shields note, "Spending by challengers is extremely effective in terms of marginal return on the percentage of the vote. First and foremost, challengers largely unknown in the district are able to use campaign spending to buy name recognition. Without gaining some unspecified threshold of name recognition, challengers are almost certain to be defeated by better-known incumbents."[3]

But campaign finance records make clear that incumbents regularly raise far more in campaign funds than challengers. The incumbents' advantage is easily demonstrated with Federal Election Commission data between 1992 and 2000. In those years, 1,820 winning House incumbents raised an average total of $654,000, compared with $228,000 raised by their challengers. The incumbents raised an average of $298,000 from PACs, the challengers $44,000. The personal funds spent by challengers averaged $51,000, while incumbents spent only $10,000.[4] This imbalance persisted after 2000. From 2000 to 2008, the average mean reelection expenditure by incumbent members of the House who won with more than 60 percent of the vote was $875,000, while their challengers spent $181,000. In closer races, where the incumbent won with less than 60 percent of the vote, the incumbent spent an average of $1,751,000, while their opponents spent an average of $940,000.[5]

The Senate numbers between 1992 and 2000 are similar. The 114 winning incumbents raised an average of $3.7 million compared to $2 million raised by their challengers. PAC contributions to winning incumbents averaged $1 million, against $177,000 contributed to challengers. In the fifteen cases over eight years where a Senate incumbent was defeated, the challenger raised an average of $7.6 million, while the incumbent raised $6.6 million. But the real power of incumbency is shown by the PAC contributions. There, the losing incumbents raised an average of $1.7 million from PACs, while the winning challengers raised only $648,000.[6] Thus, PACs continued to provide financial support for incumbents even when they were likely to be defeated. Incumbents outspent challengers on average in Senate races from 2000 to 2008. In these years, incumbent senators who won with more than 60 percent of the vote had an average mean expenditure of $4.6 million, while their challengers were able to spend only $1.2 million. In closer races, where the incumbent won with less than 60 percent of the vote, the difference in expenditures was approximately $8.8 million to $4.9 million.[7]

Breaking the financial hold of incumbents on their House and Senate seats is the most important step in creating a truly competitive election system. As in the private sector, competition improves services and responsiveness: "The freedom to choose among parties and candidates," James C. Miller III has written, "is essential to making them responsive to the electorate. Your right to switch allegiance from Carla Jones to Henry Smith is key to making Carla responsive to your preferences and making her effective in the delivery of public goods and services. Your right to abandon the Democrats for the Republicans keeps the Democrats attentive to the needs of voters (vice versa for Republicans)."[8] Mann and Ornstein see more competition as bringing forward less ideological and more moderate lawmakers in both parties: "Competitive districts and states tend to produce more moderate elected officials, ones less driven by ideological agendas and more inclined to listen to voters and groups on both sides of the partisan divide."[9]

This analysis begins to clarify why FECA and subsequent amendments placed contribution and expenditure limits on political parties. Stepping back from the individual elements of this complicated statute, we see that the most distinctive feature of FECA, followed into the BCRA, was its effort to focus fundraising and spending on the individual candidate's campaign, rather than the political party. In part, this recognized the reality that candidates could now reach voters directly through the mass media, without the network of party workers going door-to-door distributing literature. However, the mere fact that many or most candidates did not perhaps *need* or even want the help of parties was not a reason to limit the role of the parties by law. Moreover, in terms of the purported purpose of FECA—to reduce or eliminate corruption or the appearance of corruption—placing candidates in the central fundraising role made no sense at all. It's obvious, and it came to pass, that candidates and lawmakers dialing for dollars would inevitably be seen as in some way obligated to those who contributed to their campaigns.

What, then, accounts for the candidate-centric structure of FECA and its restrictions on political party expenditures? In our view, the one consistent theme in all the campaign reform legislation adopted in and after 1971 is the desire to protect incumbents. That is what caused Congress to adopt the restrictions on spending for mass media in the first version of FECA, the expenditure limits in the 1974 FECA Amendments and, in the BCRA, the soft money ban, the Millionaire Amendment, the requirement that parties choose between coordinated and uncoordinated expenditures, and the invalidation of the FEC's narrow rule on what constitutes coordinated spending. All these actions—had they been countenanced by the Supreme Court—would have gone a long way toward assuring that the campaign funds available to challengers would seldom equal the resources of incumbents, and thus that challengers would have a difficult time overcoming incumbents' inherent electoral advantages.

The Unique Role and Capabilities of Political Parties

Of a piece with these restrictions are the current limitations on contributions and coordinated expenditures by parties. These restrictions remain in current law because the Supreme Court has accepted the argument—first in *Buckley* and later in *FEC v. Colorado Republican Federal Election Committee* (*Colorado II*)—that contributions to parties can be a vehicle through which undue influence is brought to bear on party candidates for office.[10] As we have argued throughout, these restrictions favor incumbents by making it more difficult for challengers than incumbents to raise campaign funds.

One way to reduce incumbents' financial advantage would be to make both challengers and incumbents eligible for government campaign funds. That would solve a number of problems, such as the appearance of corruption associated with a candidate's direct solicitation of funds, and it would ease the burdens the current system imposes on officeholders. However, it is unlikely to address—and could exacerbate—the problem of incumbent protection. The previous chapter showed that members of Congress will consistently try to manipulate campaign finance laws to protect their own positions. This should not be surprising. Members of Congress are no different from other people; they like job security. But the consistency with which Congress has sought to create advantages for incumbents should show us that it will quickly turn any system of public campaign financing into a system of incumbent protection, probably through the simple device of equalizing amounts permitted for campaign spending. Because of its expenditure limits, such a system, similar to the public finance system for presidential campaigns, would have to be voluntary in order to meet constitutional tests. The Supreme Court has held that the presidential public finance system is constitutional only if candidates voluntarily agree to limit their spending in exchange for public financial support for their campaigns.

If such a system were adopted for House and Senate campaigns, it would be difficult for challengers to refuse public support, since they are unlikely to know in advance whether they could raise more than this amount on their own. Incumbents, on the other hand, especially those with good committee assignments and seniority, might be able to raise and spend considerably more than the limit their challenger has accepted, and they could not be constitutionally required to accept the same limit that their challenger has accepted. The result is likely to be a system not very different from what prevails today, with incumbents having inherent advantages that cannot be overcome by challengers, who would be running chronically underfunded campaigns in comparison to incumbents. Under such a system, the campaign finance laws will be frozen in place. Incumbents will not want to change a system that favors them, and challengers will not be able to attain office. It would not be extreme to suggest that the resulting semipermanent Congress is not the democratically elected Congress that the Constitution contemplates.

The best way to protect our constitutional democracy is to assure the greatest possible degree of competition for elective office, principally by making sure that the campaign finance playing field on which incumbents and challengers compete is as level as possible. This goal requires a system in which citizens themselves finance the candidates of their choice. Although establishing such a system may seem difficult at first, given the complexity of the campaign finance laws currently in place, in reality we are quite close to a workable system that achieves these results; as outlined in this and the next chapter, only a few changes are necessary.

The first and most important change would be to free the political parties from the spending restrictions in the current law that prevent them from funding the campaigns of the candidates they themselves have chosen, or who have been chosen by voters under processes the parties operate. These restrictions, which were approved by the Supreme Court in 2001 in *Colorado II*, are the most consequential pro-incumbent provisions still in the current campaign finance laws. This is because, as we show below, the parties—as permanent and continuing institutions—are uniquely situated to support challengers. In *Colorado II*, the Colorado Republican Party argued that restrictions on direct funding of a political party's candidates, or on party expenditures coordinated with candidates, violated the First Amendment by restricting the free speech rights of political parties. In a five to four decision, the Court held that, despite the strict scrutiny accorded to restrictions on speech under the First Amendment, Congress could validly conclude that contributions to a political party might be a source of corruption or the appearance of corruption, which the campaign finance laws were designed to prevent.[11] Since the decision in *Colorado II* gave deference to a congressional judgment about the effect of contributions to and expenditures by political parties, there is no reason why Congress—if it were so inclined—could not change the law to allow unlimited coordinated spending by parties on behalf of their candidates. There is nothing in *Colorado II* or in any other campaign finance decision by the Supreme Court that would be inconsistent with this outcome. As the Court noted in *Davis v. FEC*: "Congress has no constitutional obligation to limit contributions at all."[12]

Other changes in the current law could be proposed in the interest of a freer and more robust campaign finance system. Some of these were detailed in chapter 2. However, almost any change in the current law would be controversial, and apart from their conceptual deficiencies, these proposals would take many years to enact. As we argue below, so much practical good would be accomplished simply by repealing the restrictions on political parties that we recommend adopting only this change, along with a few other relatively technical changes in the current law (outlined in the introduction).

Parties as Principal Funding Sources

If campaign finance restrictions on parties are eliminated, we expect that the parties will become the principal financing sources for their candidates. This will occur for several reasons.

Parties are efficient fundraisers. The parties have the networks and the working capital to raise the funds. They can afford to hire a permanent fundraising staff, keep donor lists updated, and maintain regular contact with their donors between elections. None of these things is easy, or in some cases even financially possible, for House or Senate candidates, even incumbents. In other words, parties are more efficient fundraisers than individual candidates. The reason they have not raised more money than their candidates in the past is probably that most contributors are approached by the candidates themselves, or their representatives. If more of the fundraising chores were ceded to the parties, it is likely that they would be able to raise sufficient funds to run adequate campaigns for all their candidates. Contributors would also be more willing to contribute to parties rather than candidates if they knew that the parties were able to make most of the funds they collect—instead of just the small proportion under current law—available to the party's candidates.

The ease with which parties can now raise funds when they find it necessary is shown by the extraordinary ability of both parties in 2004 to replace with hard money—funds collected under contribution limits—the soft money banned by the BCRA in 2002. Anthony Corrado describes the highly successful adaptation of both parties to the elimination of soft money: "Both national parties . . . increased their investments in small donor solicitation programs and announced new donor programs designed to take advantage of the BCRA's higher contribution limits. . . . The DNC [Democratic National Committee] and RNC [Republican National Committee] also modified their networked fundraising efforts to accommodate the new rules. . . . The parties also benefited from their investments in improved technology. Both parties used highly sophisticated, computerized direct mail and telemarketing programs to target prospective contributors. . . . By the end of the 2004 election, the national party committee had raised more money in hard dollars *alone* than they had raised in hard and soft dollars *combined* in any previous election cycle."[13]

In the presidential election of 2008, a new phenomenon appeared that suggests a unique role for political parties in fundraising for House and Senate candidates—a role that only they can successfully perform. Barack Obama's campaign, more than any other prior campaign, demonstrated that the Internet could be a highly efficient political fundraising vehicle. The Obama campaign raised over $700 million, with a substantial portion of this total coming in over the Internet in contributions of less than $200.[14] (This was such a successful effort that it induced Obama to abandon the public financing system for the general election, forgoing an $84 million infusion of public funds.) Fundraising of this kind could only rarely be done by an individual candidate for the House or Senate. It is very unlikely that any local or state candidate would have a sufficiently large list of potential donors and a sufficiently large local or even national following to raise substantial campaign funds in this way. However, a political party, which remains active between elections, could easily build a base of Internet financial supporters to sustain the party's candidates with large numbers of relatively small donations.

Candidates will prefer party funding. Many if not most candidates and officeholders would be delighted to turn over fundraising responsibilities to their respective political parties. It is a chore that few of them like, and the need for incessant fundraising is frequently given as a reason why lawmakers retire from Congress. Once party financing becomes available, then, it is highly likely that the parties will become the principal mechanisms for financing House and Senate campaigns. Under current law, of course, it would not be in the interest of candidates to rely on party financing. The amounts that parties are able to contribute to or coordinate with their candidates' campaigns are quite small, and although there are no limits on what parties can spend independently of candidates, campaign spending experts and candidates consider such spending to be highly inefficient and frequently counterproductive.

The appearance-of-corruption issue will remain for candidates raising their own funds. The media's attitude toward campaign contributions—the simplistic idea that contributions influence the votes of lawmakers—will probably never change, and this will put pressure on candidates seeking to avoid any appearance of impropriety to allow the parties to finance their campaigns. Although the Supreme Court accepted the argument that party contributions can themselves be a back-door way for individuals and others to influence candidates and elected officials, it is highly unlikely that the public will take this idea seriously. (We look more closely at the implications of the Court's ruling in the next section.) The parties will be raising hundreds of millions of dollars, in which any individual or PAC contribution will be submerged. As John Samples noted in testimony on S. 1091, "In light of traditional categories of analysis, the corruption complaint against the parties is not persuasive. . . . If the contribution limits are actually limits on the corrupting influence of money in politics, the hard money contributions to the parties cannot corrupt."[15]

Candidates supported by parties will be more successful. It is likely that candidates who receive party contributions and party coordinated assistance will do better in elections than those who have to spend much of their time raising funds instead of campaigning. This observation will persuade increasing numbers of candidates—and especially challengers—to sign up for party financial support. The underlying idea of permitting parties to contribute to or coordinate unlimited amounts with the campaigns of their candidates is that this will enhance the chances of challengers, who always have difficulties raising the early money that is most helpful in getting a campaign staff and an advertising strategy together. With early money now available from a party, together with the technical assistance that parties will be able to offer, challengers should have a higher success rate in elections against incumbents. Once they have become incumbents themselves, the likelihood is that these candidates will continue to leave the fundraising chores in the hands of the party that originally assisted their election.

Candidates supported by parties will be able to spend more time campaigning. Challengers and incumbents who rely on party financing will be able to spend more time on their campaigns, instead of diverting campaign time to dialing for dollars. This, too, will increase the likelihood of success and may also persuade some incumbents to accept party support rather than taking the time to raise funds on their own. Once elected, candidates supported by their parties and freed from the task of fundraising will also find that they have more time to keep in contact with constituents and do a better job as lawmakers, again increasing the attractiveness of party direct contribution and coordinated spending and support. In any event, candidates elected to office with party support will not have built their own contributor base, which is essential for continued fundraising for the next election. The tendency, then, will be once again to rely on party resources when the next election comes around.

Sometimes it is argued that allowing parties to contribute unlimited amounts directly to their candidates, or to coordinate spending with their candidates, will also enhance the advantages of incumbency because parties will be induced by incumbent lawmakers to spend the sums they raise largely on incumbents. This is almost certainly incorrect. The incentives of political parties are to gain or retain political power through elections. This means defeating incumbents of the other party. Spending money on the campaigns of incumbents who are already well known in their districts or states will not advance the party's central purpose. The same thing is true of the special party committees such as the campaign committees of both parties in the House and Senate. Although these committees might be expected to spend most of their funds on the incumbents who make up their current membership, in reality the interest of the incumbents is to gain a legislative majority that will enable them to become committee chairs and otherwise enact their legislative priorities.

The Benefits of Parties as Funding Sources

There are many benefits to our political system that would follow if the political parties became candidates' primary funding source.

Reduced appearance of corruption. The principal declared motive for campaign finance reform—and certainly the motive that has been accepted as legitimate by the Supreme Court—has been the elimination of actual corruption or the appearance of corruption. In *Colorado II*, for example, the Court noted that a contribution to a political party could be a way for a contributor to circumvent the contribution limits in the law, and thus that "the choice [for the Court] is between limiting contributions and limiting expenditures whose special value as expenditures is also the source of their power to corrupt. Congress is entitled to its choice. We hold that a party's coordinated expenditures, unlike expenditures truly independent, may be restricted to minimize circumvention of contribution limits."[16] Thus, the Court's decision was based upon the notion that a person who wants to corruptly influence a candidate or officeholder could do so by contributing to a party.

With all due respect to the Supreme Court, this seems a bit far-fetched. As Justice Thomas noted, writing for the four dissenters, "The Government has failed to carry its burden, for it has presented no evidence at all of corruption or the perception of corruption. The Government does not, and indeed cannot, point to any congressional findings suggesting that the Party Expenditure Provision is necessary, or even helpful, in reducing corruption or the perception of corruption."[17] In effect, the Court majority denied a political party's First Amendment right to free speech under the somewhat questionable assumption that a contribution to a political party—already limited by the campaign finance law—*might* be used as a way of evading restrictions on contributions to candidates.

Indeed, the government's failure to show any connection between political contributions and actual voting decisions is not surprising. As we have noted repeatedly, academic research on this issue has found very little evidence that a connection exists. In *The Fallacy of Campaign Finance Reform*, John Samples summarizes the academic literature: "Social scientists have extensively studied the influence of campaign contributions on lawmaking and public policy. On the whole, they have concluded that contributions have little, if any, influence on policymaking."[18] This conclusion was based on an article by three MIT economists, who reviewed almost forty academic studies of whether campaign contributions affected voting on legislation. The conclusion of this analysis was straightforward: "The evidence that campaign contributions lead to a substantial influence on votes is rather thin. Legislators' votes depend almost entirely on their own beliefs and the preferences of their voters and their party. Contributions explain a miniscule fraction of the variation in voting behavior in the U.S. Congress. Members of Congress care foremost about winning re-election. They must attend to the constituency that elects them, voters in a district or state and the constituency that nominates them, the party."[19]

If scholars cannot find any significant evidence that campaign contributions affect the voting of lawmakers, even when the contributions are made to them directly, there is no substantial likelihood that a contribution to a political party would have any greater impact.

The remarkable thing about the Supreme Court's campaign finance jurisprudence is the ease with which the Court majority finessed the high standard of proof that is supposed to accompany any effort to limit free speech. In case after case outside the area of campaign finance, the Court has demanded strong justifications for efforts at any level of government that would interfere with speech—even speech that verges on pornography or incitement.[20] Yet, when the Court has considered campaign finance issues, it has readily granted to Congress the power to control or limit speech through the control of campaign finance, without anything more than a supposed congressional judgment that campaign contributions can induce corruption or the appearance of corruption. This approach is the more inexplicable because speech in a political context must be at the core of what the framers had in mind when they drafted the First Amendment, and because Congress has such an obvious conflict of interest—maybe even a form of corruption itself—in protecting its members against electoral challenge.

If we step back for a moment and think about the anticorruption rationale for the campaign finance laws—the rationale accepted by the Court in *Colorado II*—we find something else that is odd. A law that was supposedly intended to eliminate corruption has put candidates and officeholders at the forefront of the fundraising process. In other words, the very people we are trying to protect from corruption are placed in harm's way. How can this possibly make sense? In fact, as a matter of policy—as a matter of the purported purpose of the law—it doesn't make sense. It only makes sense as an incumbent-protection measure. Nevertheless, as long as the media continues to draw causal connections between campaign contributions and positions that lawmakers take on issues, there will always be an appearance of corruption associated with a candidate-centered campaign finance system. That is the paradox associated with this campaign finance system: it is supposed to be preventing corruption or the *appearance* of corruption, but in reality—by creating a sense of obligation in candidates—it puts candidates and officeholder into a compromised position.

Indeed, if we really wanted to protect candidates and officeholders from corruption or the appearance of corruption we would construct a system of campaign finance that did not put candidates and officeholders in the position of supplicants. Instead—assuming that we reject the idea of a government-financed campaign—we would insist that most financing come from a group that meets three tests: it has a strong incentive to support candidates, it collects funds from so many different sources that no one source could reasonably be viewed as controlling, and its purposes are broadly related to the interests of the public at large and not any narrower or special interest.

The one institution in society that meets these tests is the political party; it has the incentive and the ability to diversify its contribution base, and its interests are in the election of its candidates and the carrying out of its policies for the nation as a whole. All other groups are special interests in comparison. Considered in this light, it seems obvious that, to the extent that parties are permitted to become the principal campaign fundraising and disbursing entities for their candidates, the charge of corruption or the appearance of corruption would be substantially attenuated. Clearly, too, from the standpoint of eliminating corruption or its appearance, the worst possible structure is the current one—where the very people we want to insulate from corrupting influence are compelled to go to special interests and solicit financial support.

To be sure, the political parties could be corrupted by contributions, but this is unlikely for two reasons. First, the scope of party fundraising would be so substantial that any particular contribution would not be significant enough to buy influence; and second, parties are subject to materially different pressures than candidates. Candidates are concerned only about their own races and the politics of their districts or states. Political parties, however, "have a responsibility to a broad field of candidates and constituents, who are quick to let party officials know when they've gone too far or are otherwise out of sync with the desires and objectives of the diverse groups they represent."[21]

Reduced advantages for the wealthy. Wealthy candidates, using their own funds, are formidable candidates. One study shows a strong relationship between wealthy challengers and the defeat of incumbents: "Between 1992 and 2000, only fifteen incumbent Senators were defeated in reelection bids. Challengers spent an average of $3 million of their own money to defeat them. In elections for the thirty-eight open Senate seats during the same period, the winning candidate spent an average of more than $2 million of their own money. . . . Running for and winning a seat in the United States Senate is very much, although not exclusively, a function of personal wealth."[22] The story is much the same in the House of Representatives. There, in the eighty-six cases where challengers defeated incumbents between 1992 and 2000, the challengers contributed a total of $9.1 million to their own campaigns, while the losing incumbents contributed a total of $2.2 million.[23] Clearly, these data show why parties prefer wealthy candidates over perhaps more capable candidates who cannot afford to finance their own campaigns. Among other things, wealthy candidates can finance a campaign immediately, and don't have to wait for campaign contributions to come in. But the same data also suggest that where a party can provide adequate financing for a candidate, even an incumbent can be defeated.

Rodney A. Smith sees the preference for wealthy candidates as creating two distinct classes of candidates: "By limiting the fund-raising ability of nonwealthy candidates while ignoring the inherent advantages of incumbency and personal wealth, campaign finance reform has created two distinctly different political classes. In one class there are those who have access to personal wealth or privileged status that enables them to soak up most of the legally available dollars. Everyone else wanting to run for public office is relegated to an inferior political class to which campaign finance reform has reduced the flow of money to a trickle."[24]

In *Buckley v. Valeo*, the Supreme Court held that Congress could not constitutionally restrict a candidate's right to finance his own campaign with his own money. This decision, perfectly reasonable from the standpoint of constitutional law under the First Amendment, creates an advantage for wealthy candidates along several dimensions. First, it creates a strong incentive for parties to seek out wealthy candidates. Not only are these candidates more likely to win primaries—because of their wealth and party backing—but they are more likely to win office, too, because they are often able to compete in spending with the incumbents they are running against. As a result, lawmakers as a group are disproportionately wealthy. According to figures assembled by the Center for Responsive Politics in 2006, 34 percent of the members of Congress are millionaires.[25] Forbes reported in November 2006 that the average net worth of the members of the Senate was $8.9 million, and that about half the Senators were millionaires.[26] Obviously, there is nothing wrong with wealthy people wanting to serve the country, or using their wealth to advance their campaigns, but the current system is biased in favor of the wealthy because—at least for their first race, before they achieve the advantages of incumbency—they don't have to raise campaign funds to any significant degree, and have funds available immediately to hire the necessary staff for a full-scale campaign

This problem can be addressed only by eliminating the restrictions on party financing of candidates. The BCRA, following its incumbent-protection pattern, includes the awkward Millionaire Amendment, which allows candidates faced with "millionaire" opponents to raise more funds than the law would otherwise permit. The provision reeks of patchwork and artificiality. It seeks to plug a hole in an incumbent-protective dike. The simpler solution, by far, would be to allow parties to finance all campaigns where they believe a party candidate could win. That will have two effects—it will reduce the number of wealthy candidates chosen mainly because they are able to finance their own campaigns, and it will make funds available that will at least equal those of a wealthy candidate. Under these circumstances, nominations and offices will go to wealthy candidates only because they are the best candidates the party can recruit, not because they are wealthy.

Better candidates. Many intelligent and capable people who would make excellent candidates and lawmakers decline to run for office because they know that they will have to spend substantial portions of their time raising funds. It should be no surprise, then, that the parties today do not have the pick of the litter when they go looking for candidates in competitive districts and states. As L. Sandy Maisel wrote in 1990,

> If one is concerned about lack of competition faced by incumbents for Congress and about decisions by qualified challengers not to run for Congress, it is necessary to take a longer look at how campaigns are financed. . . . Four facts about our current campaign finance system affect the shortage of qualified candidates: (1) the total cost of campaigns has continued to rise; (2)

incumbents have little difficulty raising money; (3) challengers do; and (4) political action committees have abounded and give most of their money to incumbents.[27]

In a 1998 survey, 48 percent of political consultants rated the quality of their candidates "fair" or "poor," while only 3 percent rated their candidates as "excellent." These results continued largely unchanged in later surveys.[28] As the authors of these surveys note in a recent book, "Professional consultants—those whose access to candidates puts them in a strong position to evaluate candidates—and the general public do not believe that voters are picking leaders and representatives from the cream of the crop when they step into the voting booth on election day. Rather, they believe they are choosing from an average bunch of Americans or between 'the lesser of two evils.'"[29]

The public also believes that the need to raise funds affects the quality of the people who run for office. In another part of the same survey, respondents were asked what they thought of the statement: "It's possible that good candidates don't run for office because of the amount of money needed for a campaign." The tendentiousness of the question (anything is "possible") was probably responsible for the overwhelming result, but in any event "between 82 and 92 percent of Americans . . . thought that good candidates were foregoing elective office because of the amount of money needed to run a campaign."[30]

If the parties were able to provide financing to their candidates, it would substantially enhance their ability to recruit effective and qualified candidates. Primary elections are a generally sound way for a party to choose candidates but, as noted above, in most cases the parties have to recruit candidates to run for office. The recruitment task is very difficult. Good candidates are usually successful in other areas of life and are reluctant to leave their families and their jobs. In many cases, they can't see how they would be able to raise enough money to run a credible campaign, and in others they don't want to spend their time calling on potential donors for the funds the campaign needs. Parties with fundraising and disbursing authority would be able to assure candidates of necessary funding and thus persuade better-quality candidates to run for public office.

More time for lawmakers to do their jobs. Much of the time lawmakers spend after winning office is consumed by raising funds for their reelection.

If this burden were removed, lawmakers would have the time to review legislation, fulfill committee assignments, and otherwise improve the functioning of Congress. We are aware of no studies documenting the amount of time that lawmakers spend on fundraising, but from the anecdotal accounts of lawmakers, it appears that fundraising may rival legislative activity as a consumer of time. This is especially true for House members, who have to run for office every two years. This burden not only drives many capable people out of Congress, but it must have an adverse effect on the quality of the work that lawmakers eventually find the time to do. In a speech in 1992, Lee Hamilton, one of the most respected members of Congress at the time, corroborated this view: "Members of Congress must spend an enormous amount of time fundraising. Raising $4 million for an average Senate campaign, for example, means raising $15,000 every week over the Senator's six-year term. The money chase distorts the political process, crowding out other activities like writing laws, thinking about public policy, or meeting with ordinary voters. Incumbents know that the way to scare off competition is to raise a lot of money, and it has become a chief campaign tactic."[31]

A 2006 Supreme Court case dealt with the question of whether the time spent fundraising was a legitimate reason for restricting campaign expenditures. In *Randall v. Sorrell*, the Supreme Court reviewed a Vermont law that placed severe restrictions on campaign expenditures, and sought to justify them by arguing that the fundraising necessary to support high levels of expenditure took time away from the lawmakers' attention to their public duties.[32] This was an effort to get the Supreme Court to move away from its position that the only allowable basis for the restrictions on speech in campaign finance law is corruption or the appearance of corruption. However, the Court concluded that the *Buckley* Court had fully considered the claim that fundraising time detracted from work time, and rejected it as an acceptable reason for supporting restrictions on First Amendment free speech rights. This position, of course, would not conflict with an act of Congress that permitted parties to fund their candidates, since the effect would be to reduce the burdens on lawmakers without imposing any restrictions on the rights guaranteed by the First Amendment.

No company would stand for its employees spending substantial portions of their time on activities that have no direct relationship to what they were hired to do. Yet the American people are not getting anything like full-time service from their representatives in Congress. This situation would change if parties were permitted to make unlimited contributions to or coordinate spending with their candidates. The parties' professional fundraising staffs would be far more efficient than the candidates themselves in raising campaign funds, and lawmakers could spend their time on the things they were elected to do, rather than on trying to assemble the financial means to assure their reelection.

More efficient use of campaign funds. One of the recurrent complaints about campaign finance is that it results in too much spending. This claim is questionable, given the stakes involved,[33] but it is always raised in the context of campaign finance reform. Restrictions on campaign contributions, accordingly, are occasionally justified as a means of reducing the amount spent on a campaign. This effort, if it was really serious, has proved fruitless. Campaign spending by all participants in 2004, 2006, and 2008 set records for presidential and off-year elections. And this was after the enactment of the BCRA, which was supposed to reduce spending. If, as the Supreme Court has held, campaign spending is speech, it makes no sense to try to limit it. We should be pleased that people and parties are willing to spend as much as they do to get their views publicized and accepted.

What does make sense, however, is to make sure that campaign funds are spent efficiently—that is, that they go where they can do the most good. Parties are in the best position to judge where funds should be directed. Referring to the parties' use of their largely uncoordinated campaign spending, Sabato and Larson note: "The parties allocate the bulk of their resources to competitive contests, where they are most likely to influence the election outcome. Sure winners and certain losers are the beneficiaries of very little party support."[34]

Existing law does not allow the parties to make the most effective use of their campaign funds. The hard money funds that parties raise can be distributed to their candidates, but only in limited amounts. These funds can also be spent in coordination with their candidates, but again only in limited amounts. Although there is no limit to the amount that parties can spend in uncoordinated support for their candidates, the very word "uncoordinated" is redolent with the inefficiencies it creates. The fact that party officials cannot ask about a candidate's financial needs or the candidate's strategy for winning suggests how wasteful such spending can be.

Diana Dwyre and Robin Kolodny also note the inherent inefficiency of a system in which a party's support for its candidates is largely limited to independent or uncoordinated expenditure: "One consequence of . . . independence is that the parties make redundant outlays for polls before they will make any IE [independent expenditure] investment in television ads or mail . . . along with redundant overhead costs associated with maintaining separate office space. . . . The effort to avoid coordination between candidates and their parties is the least attractive aspect of IEs for the parties (and why they wish they could have unlimited coordinated expenditures instead!). Another consequence of independence is the possibility that the parties make campaign decisions that work against the candidate's best interests. If the candidate therefore has to campaign against the party trying to help him, money is wasted, and the voters are shortchanged by having less meaningful discourse."[35]

Finally, the current campaign finance system not only favors incumbents, but particularly favors the powerful incumbent—the committee chair, for example—who has little difficulty raising money from the PACs and individuals who agree with his use of congressional power or are interested either in currying his favor or mitigating his opposition. This results in an imbalance in the availability of campaign funds. Although all incumbents find it easier to raise funds than their challengers, incumbents who don't need vast war chests are the ones who accumulate them, and the challengers who are desperately in need of funds must go without.

Consider what would happen, then, if parties could make unlimited contributions to their candidates and coordinate spending with them without limitations. Campaign funds would be used efficiently, and spent to do the most good in light of conditions in a congressional district or state. Candidates with a chance to win would be supported, while those whose chances were limited would get only modest support. Sure winners such as powerful committee chairs and candidates without significant opposition would not receive significant allocations of party campaign funds. The current candidate-centered campaign financing regime encourages wasteful spending; a party-based system would result in more effective and efficient use of campaign finance resources.

Cheaper campaigns focused on parties' goals. The rise of consultants coincided with the decline of parties as the dominant actors in campaigns, but there has never been a satisfactory answer to why these trends occurred simultaneously. According to Dulio and Nelson, "Consultants were a reaction to, rather than a cause of party decline. . . . As parties lost some of their power, candidates were left to fend for themselves. Candidates did not have the expertise to create radio and television commercials, to conduct or analyze scientific public opinion polls, or to craft sophisticated and targeted direct mail campaigns. In other words, at the same time that parties were losing their power thanks to the spread of earlier reforms, the mode of electioneering in the United States was shifting to one in which mass communications were a primary force."[36] This is more or less the conventional explanation—that mass media electioneering reduced the importance of parties and called forth consultants to deal with the new technology.

But this does not hang together as an explanation. There is no inherent reason why the parties should lose power simply because of the rise of mass media electioneering. The parties could have supplied the same expertise that consultants came to supply, and—because of economies of scale—certainly at less cost. It is not clear why campaign spending became candidate-centered toward the end of the 1960s. But there is no question that the campaign finance laws that came in the early 1970s administered the *coup de grâce* to the parties as financing vehicles. It seems very likely that parties were prevented from rehabilitating themselves as financial sources, and had to be replaced by more expensive consultants, because FECA in 1971 and the FECA Amendments of 1974 began to restrict the degree to which the parties could coordinate activities with their candidates. It is important to recall that the FECA Amendments of 1974 set party expenditures on behalf of House candidates, whether coordinated or uncoordinated, at $5,000 per candidate for general elections, and for Senate general elections at the greater of (1) two cents multiplied by the voting age population of the state or (2) $20,000. These levels were far too low to enable parties to provide the necessary services. Providing the expertise that consultants later supplied would have been easy for parties; the problem was that they couldn't do it within the coordinated expenditure levels permitted by the campaign finance regime.

If these financing restrictions are eliminated, the parties will be able to offer—at substantially less cost—the same assistance to their candidates that consultants now offer. This change will significantly reduce the cost of campaigns, or at least lead to more efficient use of campaign funds.

But it will also have another important feature. The incentive of a consultant or campaign manager is to win; it is by winning in current races that the consultant attracts clients for future campaigns. Parties also have an incentive to win, but the party's interest is moderated by its overall philosophical foundation. A Republican candidate running with party financing will not advocate tax increases, and a Democratic candidate running with party funding will not advocate the privatization of social security. Under these circumstances, replacing an outside consultant with a party's professional staff is likely to add a policy component that will restore some meaning to political campaigns. As we will discuss in chapter 4, parties may be focused on winning, but they are likely to have a longer-term vision about policy objectives than consultants have, and are more likely to insist that their candidates stand for and support these ideological objectives. The only way these changes can occur is if the restrictions on parties' financial support for their candidates' campaigns are eliminated.

More information for voters. In his book *The Reasoning Voter*, Samuel L. Popkin argues that voters are rational in not spending a great deal of their time informing themselves about the issues or the candidates. For the most part, they have, from their perspectives, more important things to do. They process the information they get from many sources—political advertising is only one—looking for symbols and clues as shortcuts that will connect the program of a party or a candidate to their daily lives. Popkin writes: "The term *low-information rationality*, or 'gut' rationality, best describes the kind of practical reasoning about government and politics in which people actually engage. . . . Low-information reasoning is by no means devoid of substantive content, and is instead a process that economically incorporates learning and information from past experiences, daily life, the media, and political campaigns."[37]

Following Popkin, we can see parties as similar to brands in the commercial world; the party label conveys a significant amount of useful information—particularly a general idea about how a candidate of a particular party will vote if elected. But this is a clue of only limited value today. The parties have very general policies—perhaps more effectively described as attitudes or approaches—and the public is vaguely aware of what these are. But they are limited guides to what a particular candidate will actually do when elected to office. In effect, the candidate-centered campaign finance system that prevails in the United States results in 435 separate contests for the House and 33 or 34 separate Senate contests. In these circumstances, it becomes impossible for anyone to determine with any certainty exactly what it was the voters were saying when they elected a legislative majority for one of the two parties.

For the most part, despite the huge sums spent on political campaigns, voters are probably confused about exactly what they are voting for when they elect a representative or senator. And who can blame them? Candidates running their own campaigns emphasize the issues that will resonate most in their districts or states, but not in a way that connects them to any national legislative program. This makes it difficult for voters before the election to get any firm sense of how their votes for a particular candidate will translate into national policies. Even more important, after the election, it becomes difficult for a legislative majority to say they have a clear mandate to accomplish any particular political or policy objective, or for voters to hold either the elected officials or the parties themselves responsible for not achieving the goals which voters thought they were supporting.

A party-centric system of campaign finance will change this. Parties have an interest in getting their candidates elected, to be sure, but they also have powerful incentives to establish a brand—to make voters aware of what a vote for one of their candidates will mean in terms of national policies. Accordingly, to the extent that parties become a more important source of campaign finance for their candidates, there will be more useful information transmitted to voters about what their votes will mean. It is also likely that over time parties will develop national programs that will enable voters to hold them accountable if they fail to achieve promised objectives. The greater accountability of government under a party-centric campaign finance system is discussed in chapter 4.

Less power for special interests. Special interests are powerful in the United States, largely because voters hear few voices that speak for broader national interests. The national political parties potentially represent a broader perspective, but under the current candidate-centered campaign finance system, the parties are compelled to remain largely silent. This is because parties cannot achieve a consensus on policy or programs from candidates or incumbents who must depend on contributions from various special interests—or individuals with narrow perspectives—in order to finance their campaigns. There is a strong incentive not to offend, or to avoid positions that put them at odds with those whom they must later go to for campaign support.

In addition, in a very real sense, the special interests carry on the policy debate in the United States that should be carried on by the parties. This again is because the parties must defer to their candidates and officeholders. To the extent that policy proposals are developed and advanced by groups representing special interests or by the media, they are not generally endorsed by the parties, which cannot take responsibility for the effect that such an endorsement would have on the fundraising ability or electability of their candidates.

All this would change if restrictions on party funding of candidates were eliminated. In that case, candidates and officeholders—if they were willing to rely on party funding—would be able to remain independent of special interests, choosing to align themselves or not with special interest views depending on whether these were in accord with their own ideological position and that of their party. Similarly, parties would be able to develop particular policy positions that would make them participants in the policy debates that occur in connection with elections. Indeed, parties would have incentives to develop positions for which they could be held accountable by voters, much as the Contract with America—which effectively nationalized what would have been the usual series of local elections—attracted a large majority of voters to the Republican column in 1994. The salutary effect of this change would be to give voters an opportunity to hold parties and their candidates accountable for the promises made during a campaign.

Less gerrymandering. The weakening of the parties has given rise in recent decades to another phenomenon that further cements incumbents in office—the state legislative redistricting treaty that gerrymanders in-state districts so that they are solidly of one party or the other. Gerrymandering is nothing new, of course; what is new is the state legislatures agreeing to a district remapping that benefits the incumbents of *both* parties. A treaty of this kind was put into effect in California in 2001; in that case, the redistricting virtually guaranteed that of the state's fifty-four congressional seats, thirty-two would go to Democrats and twenty would go to Republicans.[38]

In general, of course, gerrymandering is not fair to the voters, but in the absence of a California-like treaty it is at least part of a competitive process. Every ten years, after the census required by the Constitution, the party that controls the state legislature gets an opportunity to increase its representation in the state's congressional delegation by revising the boundaries of the state's congressional districts in the most favorable way for its candidates. The process is competitive because over long periods each party gets a chance to make these revisions, as control of the legislature shifts back and forth. The treaty arrangement in which both parties agree to a redistricting plan that benefits their candidates is, in effect, a conspiracy against the voters, whose opportunity to elect a candidate from the other party is diminished by the gerrymander; in antitrust terms, it would be a per se illegal division of markets.

The treaty or status quo redistricting phenomenon would not happen if the national political parties were able to take control of elections by financing their candidates. The fact that parties are so weak makes a status quo treaty possible, because the electoral system then serves the interests of the most powerful forces in it—the incumbent officeholders—rather than the interests of the parties. The party's purpose is to gain and hold power; the incumbent's interest is to remain in office—even, apparently, when the price is permanent minority status. Any system that encourages the parties to seek a legislative majority in Congress must necessarily be inimical to the interests of incumbents, because the minority party must defeat as many incumbents as possible in order to become the majority. For this reason, it is not in the interest of the minority party to agree to a status quo redistricting in which it will remain in a minority position. But when the parties are weak, they do not have the leverage necessary to overcome the power of the incumbents, who have myriad ways to use federal resources to influence the votes of the state legislators ultimately responsible for the redistricting plan.

All these benefits would be achievable if parties were able to finance their own candidates' campaigns, but in the process political parties would become more powerful within our electoral system. The implications of having more powerful parties are discussed in chapter 4.

4

The Governance Benefits of Party-Centered Campaign Finance

Although we showed in chapter 3 that a party-centered campaign finance system can produce many benefits for our political and electoral system—including better candidates, better lawmakers, and more competition for incumbents—we believe it will fail as an idea unless it can be demonstrated that more powerful parties will enhance rather than detract from the quality of American government. Political parties, after all, are only a means to an end—better and more effective government, better and more effective democracy—not an end in themselves.

In his classic work, *Politics, Parties and Pressure Groups*, Professor V. O. Key succinctly described the role of political parties in a democratic system of government:

> Political parties constitute a basic element of democratic institutional apparatus. They perform an essential function in the management of succession to power, as well as in the process of obtaining popular consent to the course of public policy. They amass sufficient support to buttress the authority of governments; or, on the contrary they attract or organize discontent and dissatisfaction sufficient to oust the government.[1]

This is the customary academic view of political parties but, as this chapter shows, political parties have not always been celebrated as agents of democracy in the United States. There is a traditional American suspicion of parties—going back as far as the Federalist Papers—and it may linger unnoticed in today's politics. If parties take on a greater role in campaign finance, they

112

will inevitably become more powerful programmatic forces as well as more powerful players in the nation's politics. In this chapter, we argue that an enhanced role for our political parties will substantially improve the way our democracy works.

The American Attitude toward Political Parties

In historical and constitutional perspective, political parties in the United States have been associated with the disunity of faction and the undemocratic influence of political bosses and backroom deals. In a statement prepared just before the end of his term of office in 1796, George Washington wrote:

> The common and continual mischiefs of the spirit of party are sufficient to make it the interest and duty of a wise people to encourage and restrain it.
>
> It serves always to distract the public councils and enfeeble the public administration. It agitates the community with ill-founded jealousies and false alarms; kindles the animosity of one part against another; foments occasionally riot and insurrection. It opens the door to foreign influence and corruption, which will find a facilitated access to the government itself through the channels of party passion.[2]

It is likely that Washington's statement accurately reflected the view of political parties among the founders; we can infer this not only because there are similar critical comments on parties in Madison's famous *Federalist 10* (which refers to the "mischiefs of faction"), but also because the founders made no provision at all for parties in the Constitution or in the first ten amendments that were added in order to secure the approval of the states.

This negative view of parties remained embedded somewhere in the collective American mind, and came to the fore again in the Progressive Era, when Theodore Roosevelt and William Jennings Bryan both saw political parties as divisive instruments and obstacles to democratic change through presidential power. As discussed below, the desire to limit the power of parties extended into the 1940s, with the adoption of the Hatch Act, which limited campaign spending by the political parties and may have been the principal reason that the American campaign finance system became candidate-centered. As one modern observer notes: "Nothing is more common than the assertion that good citizens should vote for the candidate and not the party, or its corollary—that the good representative votes his or her conscience and not the party line."[3] Clearly, the implication of this frequently encountered sentiment is that the interests of political parties are different from, and possibly hostile to, the interests of the public. No wonder, then, that political parties are low in public esteem: "Public confidence in political parties lies at the bottom of the scale, lower than any other secondary association: 42.6% of respondents express 'very little' and only 3.8% 'a great deal' of confidence in them."[4]

Indeed, while a majority of voting Americans is willing to affiliate with political parties—or at least specify a party affiliation when they register to vote—parties are still regarded with suspicion. As Larry J. Sabato and Bruce Larson report in their 2002 book, *The Party's Just Begun*, "On the one hand, people recognize the civic virtue inherent in party work; on the other, they lack confidence in the parties, fail to appreciate their centrality in our system, and resist ceding their individual political prerogatives to them. The political parties have experienced a measurable decline in their legitimacy in the last quarter century. There has been a steady drop, for instance, in the proportion of people who believe that 'political parties help to make the government pay attention to what the people think.'"[5]

Even among sophisticated modern observers of the American political system, there remains an ambivalent attitude toward party-centered action. In *The Broken Branch*, Thomas E. Mann and Norman J. Ornstein describe the effects of party loyalty in Congress in two diametrically opposed ways. Describing the actions of the Republican Congress during the George W. Bush administration, Mann and Ornstein write: "The majority saw itself more as a group of foot soldiers in the president's army than as members of an independent branch of government. Serious congressional oversight of the executive largely disappeared, and longstanding norms of conduct in the House and Senate were shredded to fulfill the larger goal of implementing the president's program."[6] On the other hand, recounting events in Congress in connection with President Clinton's effort to pass a tax increase early in his administration, the authors note: "The presidential victory looked more like a defeat—it took humiliating efforts for a president to bring around individual lawmakers from his own party. . . . The new GOP strategy of trying to deny any votes for crucial president priorities, combined with the myopia of Democrats in Congress who cared less about any president's priorities than their own insular needs and viewpoints, created a public perception of a government lacking focus or the ability to act."[7] Party loyalty, accordingly, is not a good in itself, but only tolerated when it supports an objective that the observer approves.

Despite their displeasure about the way that Democrats in Congress treated a Democratic president, Mann and Ornstein's overall view is that Congress should stand up for its prerogatives as an independent branch of government and become a more significant player in the policy process. They see party loyalties and partisanship as possible obstacles to Congress fulfilling its constitutional policymaking role but also believe that strong party leadership "can help overcome the chaos and fragmentation of a legislature dominated by individuals and committees."[8]

Enhancing the power of Congress is a worthy goal, but without a sturdy party process, it seems unlikely that Congress can on its own develop a legislative program that will make it an active participant in policymaking. The modern Congress is a disparate group of 435 separately financed and elected representatives and 100 similarly elected senators, with no overall mandate to do any specific thing. Indeed, only 33 or 34 senators are elected in each election cycle. Even if all members of Congress ran for election on a platform of their own devising, they would have no power individually to enact it. The only practical way that Congress could ever assume the prerogatives for which Mann and Ornstein argue is in the presence of powerful political parties—parties that can formulate a program and require support from their members in Congress.

As we have mentioned before, one of the few examples of a successful preelection program in modern times is the Contract with America developed by Newt Gingrich and the House Republicans as a platform for the successful 1994 campaign. The Contract with America was the equivalent of a party program, and it was devised before the election so that it created a mandate for action after the election. What this seems to demonstrate is that if Congress is ever to achieve policymaking parity with the president, some unified group must develop a plan or program before an election, and get at least a majority of the candidates then running to agree to it. Only then will an election be seen to have created a mandate for action afterward.

It seems highly unlikely that a Congress could develop a legislative program *before* an election, or that a Congress elected *without* such a program could ever develop and enact its own legislative plan after the election. Large numbers of its members could certainly argue that they were not sent to Washington to do any such thing. Or their angry constituents would point this out. The only plausible mechanism for developing a legislative program that would allow Congress to operate independently of the president seems to be the political party. This is the clear lesson of developments in the American government over the past century. As the historian Joel Silbey has written: "Without the parties and what they once did for the political nation, we have returned to where we began two centuries ago . . . We have empowered chaos, and given new meaning to such terms as fragmentation, factional warfare and gridlock."9

So, while the Constitution contemplates a central role for Congress in the policymaking process, and while political parties could assist in the realization of this role, the parties have not done so in modern times. In their short history of only a little over two centuries, they have seldom had either the opportunity or the ability to enforce party discipline sufficiently for a national program of any kind. In the nineteenth century, they were too local and decentralized to come to an agreement on a national agenda; in the twentieth century, when the parties had become more national in outlook, their power was already in decline. Accordingly, while the powers of political parties have waxed and waned over time, parties have rarely performed the policy role in the United States that they routinely perform in other democracies.

The Cycles of Party Power:
A Brief History of Parties in the United States

Despite the seemingly hostile attitude of the founders toward parties, two parties developed quickly after the Constitution was ratified, with founders in each one. Although sharp and bitter personal rivalries were involved, the parties fought over the largest questions of national policy—whether, for example, the new United States would become an industrial state or remain a nation of yeoman farmers, and whether most of the sovereign power would be held by a centralized national government or by the states. The Democratic Republican party became today's Democratic Party; the Federalists gave way to the Whigs, who in turn gave way to Lincoln and the Republicans.

Through most of the nineteenth century, the parties played important roles in the electoral process—especially in choosing candidates for federal office, including the party's presidential nominee; beyond that, they were locally based institutions, the informal instruments through which local and sectional issues were brought to the formal institutions of the national government for resolution. There were a few periods when the parties had widely understood programs that the voters endorsed or rejected by electing or rejecting party candidates for office. Republican determination to hold the Union together was vindicated by victories in the important election of 1864, just as the Democratic Party's effort to build a majority behind William Jennings Bryan's populism failed with the defeat of its candidates in the realigning election of 1896.

The principal challenge to modern political parties came during the Progressive Era, beginning in the early twentieth century. Bryan among the Democrats, and Theodore Roosevelt among the Republicans, saw the locally based political parties as obstacles to achieving reform through the power of the presidency. Woodrow Wilson was a conflicted figure in this development; always a supporter of political parties, he hoped to remake the parties so that they would be instruments for the creation of a "national community," enabling the president to wield the power of the whole people. But there were strong forces in the Progressive movement opposed to party power, including the popular Theodore Roosevelt, who ran against the Republican and Democratic parties on a third-party ticket in 1912 and thus enabled the Democrat, Woodrow Wilson, to beat the Republican, William Howard Taft.

The Progressives' skeptical view of political parties fit well with the traditional American attitude, which saw parties largely as sources of faction, local interests, and dissension. The Democratic convention of 1912, where Wilson was nominated on the forty-sixth ballot, was a turning point in the history of U.S. parties. It was there that the Democratic Party endorsed the Progressive idea of nominating the president through a system of direct primary elections rather than in a convention of party professionals. In retrospect, it was probably this loss of a significant role in the presidential nomination process, together with the adoption of civil service laws and the resulting decline in party patronage power, that began the parties' long downward slide through the most of the twentieth century.[10]

Wilson's vision for a national community unified by a party was actually achieved by Franklin D. Roosevelt. Under the catastrophic economic conditions of the Depression, FDR created a coalition of many disparate—even conflicting—interests that enabled the Democratic Party to hold the presidency for twenty years, and to control Congress for most of sixty. This was the classic party organization, in which the states' rights and segregationist attitudes of its southern wing managed to coexist with the liberal values of the northern city populations, so that both could hold power and distribute its benefits to their constituencies. It's doubtful that a party embodying such conflicting political interests could exist today, but clearly political parties need not be ideologically unified in order to be effective in attaining and holding power.

After FDR, the New Deal coalition and the powerful party structure that Roosevelt had built gradually succumbed to internal conflicts. The same process occurred to a lesser extent within the Republican Party. By the early 1960s the parties had become little more than service organizations for their candidates and officeholders. As Professor John H. Aldrich noted in 1995, "The proportions and strength of party attachments in the electorate declined in the mid-1960s. There was a resurgence of affiliation twenty years later, but to a lower level than before 1966. . . . Defection from party lines and split-ticket voting are far more common for all major offices at national, state and local levels today than before the mid-1960s. . . . Elections are more candidate centered and less party centered, and those who come to office have played a greater role in shaping their own more highly personalized electoral coalitions. Incumbents, less dependent on the party for winning office, are less disposed to vote the party line in Congress or to follow the wishes of their party's president."[11]

As we indicated in the previous chapter, it is not clear why there was a turn toward a candidate-centered electoral system in the 1960s. It's worth considering the question again as we survey the history of parties in the United States. The usual explanation—that parties were weakened by the advent of mass market electioneering, that candidates did not need parties because they could now contact the voters directly through radio and television—is not really adequate.

Consider this account of the issue by Dulio and Nelson: "The great advancements in campaign technology that came about in midcentury meant that candidates could take their case directly to the people rather than be tied to a party strategy and party message. Arguably, the most important aspect of this shift was the way candidates disseminated their campaign messages to potential voters. Because candidates could no longer depend on party activity to convey their messages, as they once had, candidates began to take advantage of the new technologies that were available to them."[12] This passage well embodies the uncertainty among academics and political scientists about why parties declined. Were their candidates lured away by advances in electioneering, allowing them to take their cases "directly to the people," or were they driven away by the fecklessness of the parties? And if it was the latter, why had parties become ineffective?

Another explanation, equally unsatisfactory, is offered by Goidel, Gross, and Shields: "The effective monopoly that parties held over nominations and elections for more than 150 years was broken in the 1960s. Money and new technologies now allowed candidates to win elections without depending on political parties."[13] The question this raises is why candidates, when allowed to forgo party assistance, actually chose to do so, and why the higher costs associated with mass media electioneering were funneled to the candidates themselves in the 1960s, rather than through the parties.

It's possible that candidates always wanted to be independent of parties, and with the advent of mass media were finally able to achieve that independence, but no study seems to have documented this. The most likely explanation is that the Hatch Act of 1940—which imposed limits for the first time on party fundraising and spending—caused the parties' capabilities in campaign finance to atrophy. Thus, by the time FECA came along in the early 1970s, Senate and House candidates were already raising their own campaign funds, and understood the campaign finance benefits they reaped as incumbents. Then, with the adoption of the FECA structure, parties were frozen out of campaign finance, and hence out of a direct role in financing the electoral process. Whatever the reason, most political scientists would agree with Professor Aldrich: when political parties are weakened, "the major historical vehicle for aggregating the interests of this diverse republic, articulating them into coherent plans of action, and providing a means of holding elected officials accountable for the success or failure of their programs is all too often lost."[14]

Current Attitudes toward Parties

Writing in 2002, Larry J. Sabato and Bruce Larson professed to see encouraging growth in party strength, even to the point of advancing a party policy agenda. They attribute this growth in part to "the dwindling of the ranks of both southern conservative Democrats and northern liberal Republicans, which has made each party more ideologically and internally consistent." The two parties, they believe, now seem "able to counteract—at least to some small degree—the individualistic, atomizing forces that favor personalized, candidate-centered interest-group-responsive politics and legislative voting."[15]

Even if the parties are themselves gaining strength, however, this is not preventing the gradual deterioration in party loyalty among American voters. By the end of the twentieth century, some polls showed that a plurality of Americans regarded themselves as independents, not affiliated with any party. As Sabato and Larson themselves note, there has been a marked decline in voter-admitted partisanship: "About three-quarters of the electorate volunteered a party choice without prodding from 1952 to 1964, but since 1970, an average of under two-thirds has been willing to do so."[16] More than anything else, these facts seem to suggest that American voters are not as much hostile to parties as unable to see the value in affiliating with a party. Indeed, as long as the parties themselves—as opposed to officeholders—are not associated with any program that is relevant to voters' lives, the parties are just names, and voters have no clear reason to affiliate with either of them.

The media's attitude toward parties does nothing to help. Party loyalty is frequently treated as a kind of willful blindness, with apparently thoughtful and educated voters often quoted as saying "I don't vote for the party; I vote for the candidate," as if the party's philosophy or programs are irrelevant. Media commentary also seems to assume that bipartisanship is always good, and that legislation adopted with the support of both parties is bound to be better than legislation enacted over the opposition of the minority party. To recognize the fallacy of that approach, one need only cite the Sarbanes-Oxley Act of 2002, which passed both houses almost unanimously, but also imposed substantial costs on public companies, and drove many foreign companies out of the U.S. securities market. Bipartisan legislation has generally not received careful attention by anyone, and thus produces more than the usual number of unintended consequences.

Bipartisan legislation is also legislation for which no one is required to take responsibility. When challenged by a candidate of the other party about a vote on bipartisan legislation, lawmakers regularly defend themselves simply by citing the bipartisan character of the challenged vote. In other words, if the challenger's own party members approved the vote, how bad could it be? There is a reason why the concept of a "loyal opposition"—an institutionalized critic of the party in power—has attained such respect in Britain. Legislation inevitably picks winners and losers, and in an effective legislative process the losers' views must be fully represented.

To be sure, voters see broad differences between the parties. In general, the Republican Party is perceived as favoring smaller government, lower taxes, less regulation, and a muscular foreign policy, while the Democratic Party tends to favor a larger federal government, a larger share of national income disposed through the political process, more government regulation, and a foreign policy that emphasizes multilateral action and negotiation. Aldrich cites polls showing clear differences between the parties as perceived by the electorate.[17] Under these circumstances, it seems reasonable to conclude that the apparent weakness of the parties does not derive from a lack of identity, but from a lack of power to accomplish any particular objectives. Voters understand that there are basic differences between the parties, but do not see that parties have any practical effect.

This view is wholly rational, since today's parties have no programmatic function. They provide advice for candidates, a network, a small amount of campaign funding, and a general sense of where a candidate stands along the political spectrum, but not much else. As a result, the American people have lost sight of the value of political parties.

Political Parties and American Democracy

Whatever the American people may think about them, political parties have always had the strong support of academic specialists and political scientists.

Aldrich describes this scholarly consensus: "All agree that the political party is—or should be—central to the American political system. Parties are—or should be—integral parts of all political life, from structuring the reasoning and choice of the electorate, through all facets of campaigns and seemingly all facets of the government, to the very possibility of effective governance in a democracy."[18] Parties are especially necessary in a country as diverse as ours, Aldrich suggests, "where the problem is how to form *any* majority capable of taking action to solve pressing problems. A major political party . . . aggregates these many and varied interests sufficiently to appeal to enough voters to form a majority in elections and to forge partisan-based, majority coalitions in government."[19]

Given their essential contributions to a functioning democracy, it is understandable that scholars and others worry about the continued survival of the political parties in the United States. A CBS News poll in June 2007, for example, found that 53 percent of Americans thought there should be a third party "to compete with the Democratic and Republican parties."[20] This suggests that rather than worrying about whether the two parties will become too powerful—the result, perhaps, of giving them the power to finance their candidates—the real question is whether their continued decline will deprive our democracy of some elements essential to its effective operation.

The weakening of the political parties in the United States since the Progressive Era—a weakening that accelerated in the 1960s and was then institutionalized in the campaign finance reform laws in the early 1970s—should be a matter of concern. The two-party system in the United States must be made more relevant to the American people so that the two parties regain the confidence and loyalty of the voters.

The most effective way to bolster the parties is to provide them with the power to develop programs to present to the electorate at each election, and this in turn would require that the parties have some mechanism for enforcing party discipline among their candidates. It is at this point that the role of the parties in campaign finance becomes important. If the parties were to become the principal source of campaign finance for their candidates, they would have the leverage to assure some adherence to a party program, and to create the majority for action to which Professor Aldrich refers.

To be sure, stronger parties would inevitably engender concern about the rise of party power and the influence of party "bosses," and would raise other doubts about political parties that have always been a part of American politics. These issues should be carefully considered, but they must be weighed against the consequences of continued political party weakness. This weakness—reflected in a chronic inability to form a national majority for action—is clearly having an adverse effect on the capacity of this country to address its problems. Presidents come and go; they have a brief honeymoon with Congress before the decentralizing power of the many special interests asserts itself in opposition to the president's initiatives. In the absence of a crisis, there is no sustained pressure to develop a working majority for any particular course of action. After a brief effort, everything is deferred to the next administration.

It is this virtual paralysis in government—the collapse of consensus—that must be weighed against the fear of more power for political parties. It is important either to accept the proposition that only the parties can create a majority for action, or to suggest an alternative. Since the decline of the political parties became obvious in the 1960s, policymaking has been paralyzed. That unavoidable fact is the principal governance-related reason for strengthening the parties.

The Benefits of a Greater Policy Role for Parties

In this book, we have advanced a number of reasons why allowing parties to finance the campaigns of their candidates would have benefits for our electoral system. We have also acknowledged that a greater role in financing of campaigns will inevitably lead to more powerful parties, and particularly to parties that take a stronger role in policy formulation and implementation. With the ability to finance their candidates fully, parties will be in a position to discipline the officeholders and candidates who do not toe the party line, substantially reducing the policy independence of many of them. This will lead, in turn, to a more powerful role for parties in the process of governance.

While this role for parties is unusual in the United States, especially in modern times, it is not unusual in other democracies, and there is nothing in our Constitution that is inconsistent with strong parties that also exert some influence over the policy positions of their candidates and officeholders. In this section, we outline the benefits more powerful parties will bring, in general, to the functioning of government, and thus what benefits would flow from parties taking a greater role in policy formulation.

Continuity in policy. The erosion of party financial power that culminated in the 1960s not only placed incumbents in a stronger position vis-à-vis their challengers—as discussed in chapter 3—but also left the U.S. political process without any institution that could maintain a continuity of purpose or policy beyond a single president's administration. Although parties were never strongly programmatic institutions, they saw themselves as standing for something. As long as they had a significant role in the choice of the presidential nominee, the policies of the president and the party were hard to distinguish. But as primaries and local caucuses became more important, parties gradually lost their ability to choose their presidential candidate, and they also ceded their policy role to the presidential candidate chosen for them by the voters.

Thus the policies of the president became the policies of his party, and if a party did not control the White House it simply had no policymaking apparatus and no coherent policies. Even in cases where a party had elected a president, the policies that were the reason for his election, and that had animated his administration, were simply packed off with his files at the end of his term in office. The next president, even of the same party, started with a clean slate. The absence of parties from the policy field also affected Congress, which—without any institutionalized system for the development of a program to take to the American people before an election—was unable to serve as a policy counterweight to the president. This was especially true if the majority party in one or both houses of Congress did not also control the White House; the only viable strategy for a house of Congress that had no coherent program of its own was to oppose or frustrate the president's program. Mann and Ornstein make this point: "The presidency gained enormous power during much of the twentieth century, particularly over national security, and public expectations about what the occupant of the White House could and should accomplish soared. Congress in turn was increasingly judged by whether it facilitated or frustrated the president's agenda."[21]

Because parties are the only informal national political institutions that survive from presidential administration to presidential administration, the loss of any party role in policy meant the loss of policy continuity. This loss in turn made change far more difficult to achieve. The Constitution sets up a system of checks and balances that permits change to occur, but only slowly over time. It's a brilliantly conceived structure for protecting the individual against government encroachment, but moving the system to accommodate change seems to require steady pressure over many years. With the president the only source of policy initiatives, and without political parties to carry forward ideas beyond a single presidency, it becomes difficult to accommodate government policies to major changes in economic conditions or technology.

Without some strong source of party discipline, it is impossible for a political party to create a program on which its candidates can run. The inclination of candidates will always be to preserve their independence and their ability to choose the terms on which they will stake their election. This is understandable, and in most cases unexceptionable, but candidate independence is a prescription for continued weakness in congressional policy-making, and that in turn promises a continued lack of a policy mandate for elected officials. Thus, to the extent that permitting political parties to fund the campaigns of their candidates will enable them to create and enforce party discipline, one clear benefit will be to provide continuity in political party positions from administration to administration. This continuity will make change easier to achieve in the American constitutional system.

Choice in public policy. Despite the ambivalence of the population at large, political parties have always had supporters outside politics itself, especially in the academic community. The strongest advocates of party government have frequently been political scientists and professional students of government. One such student, Woodrow Wilson, wrote in his doctoral thesis in 1885 that "parties should act in distinct organizations, in accordance with avowed principles, under easily recognized leaders, in order that the voters might be able to declare by their ballots, not only their condemnation of any past policy, by withdrawing all support from the party responsible for it; but also and particularly their will as to the future administration of the government, by bringing into power a party pledged to the adoption of acceptable policy."[22]

Wilson was arguing that parties should be far more powerful than they have ever been in the United States, but he was also pointing to one of the key benefits of political parties: providing voters with a choice. In 1950, a committee of the American Political Science Association issued a report entitled *Toward a More Responsible Two-Party System*.[23] The committee, made up of some of the most respected political scientists of the day, called parties "indispensable instruments of government," and went on to affirm that "popular government in a nation of 150 million people requires political parties which provide the electorate with a proper range of choice between alternatives of action. . . . The crux of public affairs lies in the necessity for more effective formulation of general policies and programs and for better integration of all of the far-flung activities of modern government."[24]

This statement concisely summarizes the potential role of a party in providing the electorate with a choice, and is known to political scientists as the "responsible party doctrine." The role envisioned for the party cannot of course be performed by a single senator or representative, who can tell his constituents what he will support but not promise them that it will be accomplished if he's elected. The president can come closest to making this promise, but even he must negotiate his program with Congress after his election, and in many cases the president's program is not enacted or, if enacted, comes out in a barely recognizable form.

How, then, without parties that offer a choice, does the public make its will known? The answer is: with difficulty. Every four years, the American people elect a president, and if his majority is large enough, and he has been clear enough about his intentions, he is said to have a mandate. But unless the new president is seen as responsible for his party achieving a majority in Congress, he must contend with the fact that most of the members of Congress owe him nothing and are more concerned about the needs of their own constituencies than his success. Since they are the ones who have to raise the funds for their reelection, they must also keep in mind the fact that their constituents and financial supporters may have different views than they about the president's program; and for members of Congress, constituent and financial support is likely to be more persuasive than the ties of party loyalty.

Thus, with each candidate running independently, even though under a party label, it is difficult to tell what an election means. One party may have acquired a majority in the House, Senate, or both, but what does this victory mean? What have the people really voted for, and what kind of mandate have they provided? These ambiguities are among the most significant reasons that our government moves so slowly—or not at all—to address pressing problems. In reality, when the American people vote, they send a very mixed message. They elect a president who may have a personal program, but they also elect a Congress that is fractionalized along numerous lines and that has many different ideas about the national welfare. How can anyone determine in such a system what the American people have voted for? How can a majority for action be developed in this political environment?

Strong political parties can bring clarity to this question. Parties have always been capable of developing a set of programs and policies as a platform for a presidential campaign. Despite the widespread view that these documents are filled with meaningless generalities, that is not the case. As Sabato and Larson note in comparing the Democratic and Republican platforms in 2000, "On a host of issues, the two parties could not have taken more divergent substantive positions—and there is nothing mushy or tepid about the rhetoric employed, either." They add that "the 2000 platforms were not exceptional in this regard," and they cite a study showing that between 1944 and 1976, the parties' platforms "were consistently and significantly different."[25]

Admittedly, the platforms are aspirational in nature rather than true programs for action. But a comprehensible and comprehensive party program, drawing upon the aspirational elements of its platform, could impose a great deal of order on the chaotic system that now prevails in U.S government policymaking. Unfortunately, within the current candidate-centered campaign finance system, the political parties do not have sufficient leverage with their own candidates to induce their support for either the quadrennial platform or any other set of policies and programs.

In a well-functioning party system, the parties would offer a program. If they gain a legislative majority, they have been given a mandate to enact their program. If their program fails to meet the objectives they set out for it, they bear the responsibility, just as they must if they fail to enact their program at all. In both cases, they risk being turned out of power at the next election.

It should be clear that parties can adopt programs and get them enacted. So too can party members working in concert, such as we saw when the House Republicans promoted and passed their Contract with America. It would have been just as easy for the Republican Party outside Congress to adopt the Contract with America, but the party has not for nearly a century seen itself as a policy-formulating institution, and its effort to adopt a program probably would have been opposed by elected officials. Nevertheless, the Contract presented the voters with a clear choice, and it shows that a multifaceted program can be formulated by, and form the base of an election campaign for, a group with the power to enact it. Certainly a party with the power to finance its own candidates would have the necessary leverage to gain the support of its candidates for such a program.

Fostering of accountability. Developing programs that provide a choice for voters is one thing; taking responsibility for enacting a program and for its success is another. As Sabato and Larson note: "Accountability without parties is impossible in a system as multifaceted as America's. After all, under the separation of powers arrangement, no one—not even the president—can individually be held responsible for fixing a major problem because no one alone has the power to do so. Collective responsibility by means of a common party label is the only way for voters to ensure that officials are held accountable for the performance of the government."[26]

The current electoral system in the United States makes it very difficult for voters to hold politicians accountable and assign responsibility for political failure. In federal elections, the voters elect representatives and senators, but the connection between the policies of these lawmakers and actions by Congress is highly attenuated. This is because the power of an individual lawmaker is very small, and the ability to get legislation adopted singlehandedly is virtually nonexistent. Accordingly, how is a voter to know whom to hold accountable if, despite the election of the person he voted for, nothing happens in Washington? The senator or representative elected with the support of a majority of voters can easily point out that he is only a single lawmaker, and unable, without the support of a majority of the Senate and House, to get legislation adopted. Anyone who has ever heard a member of Congress denounce the failings of Congress in a speech to his constituents knows exactly what is going on. Under these circumstances, responsibility is diminished or lost. As Aldrich notes: "No one person either can or should be held accountable for actions taken by the House, Senate, and president together. The political party as a collective enterprise, organizing competition for the full range of offices, provides the only means for holding elected officials responsible for what they do collectively."[27]

This failure of accountability will never be resolved until political parties begin to develop their own programs and go before the American voters with a promise to adopt certain legislation if the party is given a legislative majority. As Woodrow Wilson suggested, the parties—and only the parties—are in a position to offer the voters a meaningful choice in what they want Congress to do. The choice of a president is binary—that is, there are generally two candidates, and the voters have an opportunity to choose between them along the dimensions of policy, personality, and background. When a president is elected, voters have a reasonably good idea of where he wants to take the country. The choice for the Senate or the House of Representatives is far more complicated; the voters have no idea, when they elect a representative or senator, what Congress as a whole will ultimately do, or they have only the most general idea of how their votes will produce a particular result. There is no effective way, in other words, for voters to hold individual senators and representatives accountable for the failure to enact the legislative program that the candidate offered to the voters during the election process.

This is a significant problem in the U.S. constitutional system, because the system works effectively with only two parties and thus, unlike parliamentary systems, does not create a significant voice or bargaining unit for the voter who is strongly interested in a particular policy. In multiparty systems, the necessity for party coalitions gives voters a much more clearly articulated and effective way to affect national policy than is true of a two-party system. This deficiency, however, can be corrected by elections in which the parties themselves are held accountable. Thus, strengthened political parties—parties that promise the voters a series of programmatic results if they are given power, and that can be defeated if the results are not forthcoming—provide the electorate with a meaningful choice. Voters would then have a better idea of what to expect if they vote for the candidates of a party. And they could hold the party accountable far more easily than their representative or senator, who obviously does not have the power by himself to enact needed legislation.

Nor would stronger parties necessarily diminish the power of the presidency. In our constitutional system the president is a major player in the policy process, and can be of a different party than the one that controls Congress. In that case, there is further bargaining, and the president and his party will have to take their chances on opposing the programs of a party that has won a legislative majority. In reality, as occurs today, the outcome is likely to be a compromise, with both sides—the president and Congress— claiming to have fulfilled the mandate received from the voters. But at the next election, the voters will have an opportunity to decide whether this was true from their all-important perspective.

If the president is of the same party as the congressional majority, that will ease the process of getting his legislative package adopted. His window for success will not be limited to the "first hundred days," before the drama of his election and inauguration is exhausted and Congress begins to fracture again along traditional lines. The president's program, of course, will have been vetted with his party—will become the program of the party—before the election, so there will be little question about who is responsible if the program is not adopted. And yet, if the program ultimately adopted is not satisfactory to the voters, there will be another congressional election two years later, where the opposition party will be able to present its contrasting set of initiatives.

Aggregation of special interests. Stronger political parties would have an important role in aggregating a wide variety of special interests into a coalition. If our government functions effectively with only two parties, then each of them has to include within it a huge number of special interests that demand representation at the national level.

The American Political Science Association report on the party system was prompted by what was seen, even then, as a decline in the role of parties in the American political system. Addressing the question of integrating special interests into a broader program for the nation as a whole, the committee recognized the crucial role parties play: "By themselves, the interest groups cannot attempt to define public policy democratically. Coherent public policies do not emerge as the mathematical result of the claims of all the pressure groups. The integration of the interest groups into the political system is a function of the parties. Any tendency in the direction of a strengthened party system encourages the interest groups to align themselves with one or the other of the major parties."[28]

This suggests that strengthened parties will reduce the tendency of special interests to capture officeholders. To the extent that these interests believe that their priorities can be enacted through the parties, they will not press their views as aggressively on individual officeholders. Correlatively, if a successful party can enact its program, the special interests will not be able to gain much traction in Congress for policies and programs that have not been adopted by one of the parties. Thus increasing the power of the parties by giving them a stronger campaign finance role will help focus special interests on the political parties rather than on the candidates and officeholders. Subsuming special interests within the larger national coalition of interests represented by the parties will make the adoption of legislation much easier; Congress will not appear—as it often does today—incapable of resolving difficult issues of policy. If the president's program is different from that of the party that controls Congress, bargaining will ensue, but in this case there is a greater likelihood that an agreement reached between the leaders of Congress and the president will actually be implemented in legislation.

Some might worry that with campaign contributions increasingly going to the parties, parties are at risk of being corrupted. But as we suggested in the previous chapter, there are great and important differences between the influence that can be brought to bear on a party through a campaign contribution and one that can be brought to bear on a particular lawmaker. The position of the party as a broad-based institution that is raising substantial amounts of money for a national campaign immediately attenuates the influence of any single contribution. Any contribution is likely to be lost in the huge sums that the parties will be able to raise from many different constituencies. In addition, the party, unlike the individual candidate, has an interest in winning nationally, and to do so must assemble a broad coalition of interests. Tilting toward any particular special interest will impair this balancing process. In other words, if political parties are given the power to develop policy and programs, they will be able to reduce the power of special interests, not be swayed by it, and be more likely to develop a broad national program of legislative action.

Support for governmental initiatives. Of necessity, a program advanced by a party will be skeletal in nature. The devil, as they say, will be in the details, and these will come to light and be worked out through hearings and informal consultations with affected interests. Indeed, even party initiatives that attracted considerable support in a past election can easily lose support as the compromises required for legislation in a pluralistic society are stitched together.

In the end, however, if a legislative initiative emerges, the American people will have to be able to see it as a fulfillment of the mandate they gave. If the president is on board, a substantial proportion of this task will have been accomplished, but even with the support of the president it may be difficult to build the consensus among major groups that controversial legislation requires. A unified position by the sponsoring party and its members will be essential in that effort. The members are a ready-made core coalition around which the necessary national support can be organized. Stronger parties—parties which the American people understand to have some direct relationship to policies, programs, and governance—will be able to enlist far more interest from the electorate. Sidney Milkis notes that in the past, "political parties . . . played a critical part in linking private and public concerns, as well as local loyalties and national purpose."[29] If sufficiently strengthened through the ability to finance the campaigns of their candidates, this is the role they could play once again.

Conclusion

We have shown in this chapter the benefits that would flow to our democracy if political parties were able to finance and exert more influence over their candidates and officeholders. The most important of these is to provide a mechanism with which the electorate can hold their representatives accountable and fix responsibility for failure. But other benefits would be almost as important: the power of special interests would be diminished; the voters would have a clearer sense of what the parties would do if they gained a majority; and the parties, by carrying their policy focus over a longer period than simply a single presidency, would be able to provide a more stable and consistent set of programs. In addition, the parties would have a continuing and institutional interest in educating the American electorate on the benefits of the programs they are advancing, and thus mobilizing support for initiatives that would otherwise lie dormant.

Weighed against these advantages is, at bottom, the traditional American fear of concentrations of power. Many Americans will reject the idea of more powerful parties because of concern that this will give unelected party bosses great power over the government's policies. But this is like saying that unelected CEOs, rather than consumers, determine whether a product is successful in the market. The central fact associated with political parties is that they are interested in only one thing—gaining and holding political power. In a vigorous democratic system, competition between the parties for the support of the voters should ensure that the parties' influence over their candidates and officeholders will advance the voters' interests.

Conclusion: Now, It's Up to Congress

In this book, we have attempted to show that a more party-oriented campaign finance system would serve a number of important purposes, including a more competitive electoral system, greater accountability of parties and candidates, the attenuation of concerns about undue influence or corruption, and more coherence to our frighteningly complex campaign finance laws.

In previous chapters, we have described efforts by Congress to use the campaign finance laws to create obstacles for challengers, and the actions of the Supreme Court in striking down most—but not all—of these. What is left is a mare's nest of restrictions, exclusions, exemptions, and allowances that is both a trap for the unwary and an unmanageably complex, incumbent-protective legal regime that accomplishes none of its stated purposes. Congress would do well to consider whether it does not owe the American people a more honest system for financing political campaigns in what is still the greatest democracy in the world.

The simple irrationality of the current system makes our point. Since the enactment of the BCRA, our national political parties must carry on all their activities with hard money. This means that the money a political party committee raises is limited in amount, must be fully disclosed (above the most modest threshold of $200), comes only from individuals (not corporations, unions, foundations, or other similar entities), and comes in amounts and under conditions prescribed by Congress or approved by the Federal Election Commission.

These restrictions on political parties—for no sound policy reason that is apparent—put them at a distinct disadvantage compared to other powerful players in the political system that do not have to play by those same restrictive rules. Almost immediately after the BCRA took soft money away from parties, a group of "shadow parties"—the 527s—arose as serious political players. These entities can do almost everything parties can do—including the financing of issue advertising and organizing get-out-the-vote campaigns—but with less disclosure and less accountability; and they can take money from corporations, unions, foundations, and similar entities forbidden to candidates and political parties. Thus the effect of the BCRA was to diminish the importance of the political parties in the electoral process and to empower competing organizations that are not subject to the same restrictions on how and from whom they can raise funds. In the 2004 election cycle, for example, a mere twenty-four individuals contributed an astounding total of $142 million to 527s—an amount that was approximately 20 percent of the sum raised by both major political parties—and the spending by these wealthy individuals inevitably affected the outcome of the election. One Supreme Court justice noted the irony that a law intended to take the "fat cats" out of politics just herded them to a less visible location and made them relatively more powerful.[1] Under these circumstances, can anyone really question that this outcome is irrational?

Then there are the continuing restrictions on the ability of our national parties to use hard money to support their candidates, an issue that we have raised again and again in this book. Even within the distorted goals of the campaign finance regime itself, this is an incoherent restriction—unless of course we simply admit that the purpose of the campaign finance system is to protect incumbents. At the outset, it is important to recognize that the reason hard money contributions have a maximum size in the first place is that Congress has asserted that a contribution up to this amount will not cause corruption, the appearance of corruption, or undue influence. So why is it, then, leaving aside the protection of incumbents, that a party permitted to raise only hard money cannot use as much of these funds as it wants to aid the campaigns of its candidates? If the party is not deemed by Congress to be unduly influenced or corrupted by the hard money contributions it is permitted to receive, how can these contributions then be said to corrupt or unduly influence the *candidates* for whom the party uses these funds? It is important to keep in mind in this connection that it is illegal under the FEC's regulations for a party donor to earmark the funds for a particular candidate.

Nevertheless, several years ago, a bare five to four majority of the Supreme Court—disregarding the law's explicit prohibition against earmarking contributions for specific candidates, and Congress's obvious conflict of interest—upheld the current restrictions on a party's support for its candidates.[2] The hypocrisy of Congress in this case is demonstrated in the BCRA's famous Millionaire Amendment, which provides that when candidates face a challenger who has made a contribution of $350,000 or more to his own campaign, the restrictions on party coordinated expenditures are eliminated and the parties are able to assist their candidates (who will, of course, usually be incumbents) until the challenger's financial advantage is overcome. By this measure, Congress communicated that it well understands the power of the political parties to provide campaign funds, but just wants that power limited in cases where it might be used to assist challengers.

Finally, there is the ultimate absurdity, the fact that although contributions directly to candidates are limited to $2,300, the law also permits the use of "bundlers," who collect the contributions of large numbers of individuals and deliver them directly to candidates. Clearly, this provision destroys the notion that limiting contributions to candidates reduces the appearance of corruption or undue influence. Let us hasten to add that we are not opposed to bundlers; they are simply another demonstration of the central inconsistency of the campaign finance laws we have today, in which the same contribution limits that are supposed to insulate candidates from undue influence require candidates to go hat in hand to the very people who supposedly want to corrupt them.

Even if there were a legitimate concern that removing the limits on a political party's ability to contribute to or coordinate expenditures with its candidates creates the possibility of corruption or circumvention—recall that it is illegal for a donor to earmark funds for a particular candidate—there are simpler ways to address the issue. For example, a great deal of party hard money comes in the form of very small donations, averaging $50 annually, as well as from those who give much more. Parties could be permitted to set up a special fund for all contributions of $2,300 or less and then use only those funds to engage in coordinated expenditures with their candidates. This would enhance the value of smaller contributions, eliminate any realistic concern with corruption/circumvention, and better enable parties and candidates to help their candidates through coordinated election spending.[3]

Unfortunately, while the current campaign finance system is irrational and absurd in many ways, it is wholly rational in one: from the perspective of incumbents, even with all the losses they have suffered at the Supreme Court, the current system works exactly as designed. The major threat they face has always been the ability of the parties to raise the funds for challengers and hence to create a truly competitive electoral system. That's why parties have been limited to hard money, and why their ability to assist their candidates through coordinated expenditures or direct contributions has been severely limited. In our introduction, we recorded the serious adverse consequences for our electoral system of a candidate-centered campaign fundraising regime, including its tendency to place candidates in the position of supplicants, to favor wealthy candidates, to prevent good potential candidates from running for office, and to deny the American people the information they need to make good choices as voters. Most particularly, we noted that the candidate-centric system protects incumbents by limiting contributions and coordinated spending by parties to approximately 1 percent of what campaigns actually cost on average, and—because challengers always have a more difficult time raising funds than incumbents—thus prevents the development of a truly competitive electoral system.

In chapter 1, we outlined how the restrictions on parties were merely one of a number of incumbent-protective devices that Congress adopted in the name of campaign finance "reform," and showed by this that the restrictions on parties were no accident or unintended consequence. Rather, the party restrictions just happen to be the one surviving relic of a series of efforts—mostly involving expenditure limitations—that members of Congress adopted between 1971 and 2002 with the obvious purpose of protecting their own positions. As a result, as almost everyone who follows elections in this country knows, the reelection rate of incumbents is a scandalously high 98 percent in many years. Is it any wonder that only 14 percent of the American people say that they approve of what Congress is doing, while in each election they reelect over 90 percent of its members?

In chapter 2, we discussed alternatives to our approach, which would free the political parties from the restrictions on their ability to finance their candidates, and we noted that all the alternatives—if current state and local laws are any guide—would result in more incumbent protection in the name of "reform." Public financing systems, the most popular kind of reform, have failed to prevent incumbent protection, and in some cases have to be linked with term limits in order to overcome the incumbent advantages that the incumbents themselves—with the support of campaign finance reformers—have written into state and local laws. These systems are incumbent-protective in that they almost always limit campaign spending, and that practice hands advantages to incumbents, who have myriad ways to advertise themselves and their good works through the necessary communications with their constituents. For that reason, we pointed out, if we are to have a truly competitive electoral system, challengers must have the ability to raise more funds than incumbents—and that can realistically happen only if challengers are themselves wealthy enough to finance their own campaigns or if they are helped by the political party that nominated them.

In chapter 3, we reviewed the many ways in which a party-centric fundraising system would benefit the American people and our democracy. It would do so, we showed, primarily through creating true electoral competition and electoral accountability of the parties themselves. We outlined how the elimination of the candidate-centric regime—and the substitution of a regime that relied on parties to raise campaign funds and support their candidates—would address each of the serious deficiencies in our current system discussed in the introduction. Such a regime, we noted, would not require the abandonment of contribution limits—although some of the limits would have to be changed in order to encourage more contributions to parties—but would lift only the current restrictions on the ability of the political parties to provide financial assistance directly to their candidates or to coordinate expenditures with them.[4]

Finally, in chapter 4, we addressed the one significant question that we think is raised by our proposal—the likelihood that the parties would become far more powerful in the American political system than they have been since the beginning of the last century. There is a historic strain in American politics, extending from the founders through the Progressive movement of the early twentieth century, that distrusts political parties. This distrust, sharpened by media images of smoke-filled rooms and corpulent party bosses, is widespread today, but it is not shared by political scientists. Scholars and students of government have long argued that more powerful parties would allow the American people to express their views more effectively and make our constitutional system work better. In chapter 4, we showed how these benefits would outweigh any concerns about increasing the power of the political parties.

Because the Supreme Court has ruled that restrictions on parties' contributions and coordination with their candidates are constitutional, the only recourse is to prevail upon Congress to change the law. As difficult as this will be (given that current law heavily favors incumbents), it is the only way that our electoral system can be made more competitive and the benefits of that competition made available to the American people.

As it happens, legislation has been introduced in both the House and Senate to accomplish this purpose. The first of these bills, introduced in the House in June 2005 by Mike Pence, a Republican, and Albert Wynn, a Democrat, and designated HR 1316, would have eliminated restrictions on party funding of, or coordination of expenditures in, political campaigns. Unfortunately the bill immediately became entangled with the issue of restricting 527s, which had in 2004 provided $360 million in support of Democrats and $85 million in support of Republicans.[5] As a result, the bill came to be looked upon as an effort by the Republicans to rein in 527s, and was opposed by the Democratic leadership in the House and editorially by the *Washington Post* and the *New York Times*. Nevertheless, the bill was voted out of committee in June 2005 and in April 2006 was endorsed by Senator John McCain,[6] but it was never adopted by the full House.

In April 2007 the Senate Rules Committee held hearings on S. 1091, the Campaign Accountability Act of 2007, introduced by Senators Robert Bennett (R-UT) and Robert Corker (R-TN), which would have provided a simple, straightforward, even elegant step toward a more party-centered campaign finance regime.[7] The bill would have repealed the current statutory limits on the amount of money that party committees can spend in coordination and consultation with their candidates. Particularly noteworthy is the fact that the bill was actively supported not just by the usual deregulatory groups, but also by certain key campaign finance analysts and political scientists, including Thomas Mann, who supported the BCRA's ban on national parties' use of soft money, and Michael Malbin, who heads the nonpartisan Campaign Finance Institute.

In his testimony before the Senate, Mann argued that eliminating restrictions on party coordinated spending was necessary in order to assure that parties and candidates both took responsibility for campaign advertising. When parties are forced to make their expenditures independently, the candidate does not take responsibility for what the party might say:

The 2004 and 2006 elections confirmed a new reality regarding party financing of federal elections: there is no limit on what parties can spend in hard dollars for their candidates in federal elections, only restrictions on the legal form of those expenditures. Parties can make limited contributions to candidates, limited coordinated expenditures spent with candidates, and unlimited independent expenditures. . . . The idea of a political party spending independently of its own candidates, affirmed in *Colorado I*, strikes most political scientists as preposterous, especially once the party's nominee is selected. What public good is served by forcing parties to set up entirely independent operations, which avoid any coordination with that candidate? It is a perversion of the whole purpose of political parties.[8]

Noting that parties spent approximately $250 million in both the 2004 and 2006 election cycles, Mann concluded that the costs of the present system "are diminished efficiency and accountability." Eliminating the coordinated expenditures limitations, he argued, would secure the advantages of efficiency and responsibility, without compromising BCRA's prohibitions on corporate and union contributions to parties, its limits and restrictions on the amount and use of individual contributions, and requirement of full disclosure. Rather than undermining any reform values, repealing the limits on hard-money coordinated spending by parties "would . . . strengthen ties between parties and their candidates, increase the accountability of candidates for party-financed campaign activities, and improve the efficiency of party operations. The latter might have the desirable side effect of encouraging the parties to target their resources in a less concentrated fashion, thereby expanding the number of seriously contested races."[9]

As the Mann testimony makes clear, the limits on coordinated party/candidate expenditures serve no meaningful purpose in terms of preventing parties from becoming channels or conduits for corruption, but they do undermine the ability of candidates and parties to work together to further electoral responsibility and democratic values. Continuing to impose such restrictions in the current campaign finance world makes no sense, and for that reason borders on invidious discrimination against political parties and their members and candidates. As Chief Justice Roberts said in response to the claimed need for endless vigilance against all forms of circumvention of campaign contribution limitations: "Enough is enough."[10]

In the same hearing, Michael Malbin—speaking on behalf of himself as a scholar, and not as the head of the nonpartisan Campaign Finance Institute—made an equally important point. With only fully disclosed, source-sanitized, amount-limited hard money going into the parties, there is no gain in corruption prevention to put any restraints on how the party spends that money:

> So after McCain-Feingold, why limit party spending? . . . The wisdom of these limits has become particularly hard to defend after the Supreme Court's decisions in *Colorado-I* and *McConnell v. FEC.* In both cases, the Court said the parties have a constitutionally protected right to make unlimited independent expenditures using hard money. The question is: if unlimited independent spending is a given, why not allow unlimited coordinated spending? . . .

> Now that the contributions have been limited after BCRA, the question is whether candidates and parties should be able to work together on their election ads, as they used to do. I would say yes. . . . I think that once you have contributions under control, the more accountable spending is better. Candidates who run on a ballot under a party label are the parties' candidates . . . These party labels are still the most important cues voters use to help process information during a busy election season. It does the democratic process no good when we blur those lines by requiring the parties' messengers and candidates to stay at arm's length.[11]

Our campaign finance system is now seriously broken. Although it may not be in the interest of incumbents to fix it—that is, to eliminate the current restrictions on what the parties can do to assist their candidates—there is no question that the necessary repairs are a *responsibility* and *obligation* of our senators and representatives. Now, it's up to Congress.

Notes

Introduction and Summary

1. See *Buckley v. Valeo*, 424 U.S. 1 (1976).

2. *FEC v. Colo. Republican Fed. Campaign Comm.*, 518 U.S. 604 (1996) [*Colorado Republican I*].

3. *FEC v. Colo. Republican Fed. Campaign Comm.*, 533 U.S. 431 (2001) [*Colorado Republican II*].

4. See, e.g., Thomas E. Mann, testimony, Senate Committee on Rules and Administration, *Repealing the Limitation on Party Expenditures on Behalf of Candidates in General Elections* [S 1091], 110th Cong., 1st sess., April 18, 2007, http://rules.senate.gov/hearings/2007/041807Mann.pdf (accessed September 18, 2008).

5. Ibid., 3.

6. Campaign Finance Institute, "Table 3-12: Political Party Contributions, Coordinated and Independent Expenditures for Congressional Candidates, 1976–2008 (in dollars)," "Table 3-2: House Campaign Expenditures, 1974–2008 (net dollars)," and "Table 3-5: Senate Campaign Expenditures, 1974–2008 (net dollars)," forthcoming, http://www.cfinst.org/. Data provided to authors by Campaign Finance Institute executive director Michael Malbin in February and March 2009.

7. Ibid.

8. Anthony Corrado and Katie Varney, *Party Money in the 2006 Elections: The Role of National Party Committees in Financing Congressional Campaigns* (Washington, DC: Campaign Finance Institute, 2007), 17, http://www.cfinst.org/books_reports/pdf/Corrado_Party-2006_Final.pdf (accessed September 18, 2008).

9. Senator Ted Stevens, opening statement, Senate Committee on Rules and Administration, *Repealing the Limitation on Party Expenditures on Behalf of Candidates in General Elections* [S 1091], 110th Cong., 1st sess., April 18, 2007, http://rules.senate.gov/hearings/2007/041807correctedTranscript.pdf (accessed September 18, 2008).

10. *Bipartisan Campaign Reform Act of 2002*, Public Law 107-155, § 214(a), 107th Cong., 2nd sess. (March 27, 2002), http://frwebgate.access.gpo.gov/cgi-bin/getdoc.cgi?dbname=107_cong_public_laws&docid=f:publ155.107.pdf (accessed September 18, 2008)(codified at 2. U.S.C. §441a(a)(7)(B)(ii)(2005)) .

11. Trevor Potter, "The Current State of Campaign Finance Law," in *The New Campaign Finance Sourcebook*, ed. Anthony Corrado, Thomas E. Mann, Daniel R. Ortiz, and Trevor Potter (Washington, DC: Brookings Institution Press, 2005), 55.

12. Campaign Finance Institute, "Table 3-6: Expenditures of Senate Incumbents and Challengers, by Election Outcome, 1980–2008 (mean net dollars)," forthcoming, http://www.cfinst.org/. Data provided to authors by Campaign Finance Institute executive director Michael Malbin in February 2009.

13. Campaign Finance Institute, "Table 3-3: Expenditures of House Incumbents and Challengers, by Election Outcome, 1974–2008 (mean net dollars)," forthcoming, http://www.cfinst.org/. Data provided to authors by Campaign Finance Institute executive director Michael Malbin in February 2009.

14. See *Federal Election Campaign Act of 1971*, Public Law 92-225, 92d Cong., 2d sess. 86 Stat. 3 (February 7, 1972); and *Federal Election Campaign Act Amendments of 1974*, Public Law 93-443, 93d Cong., 2nd sess. 88 Stat. 1263 (October 15, 1974)(current version codified at 2 U.S.C. §§ 431 et seq.).

15. 424 U.S. 1 (1976).

16. Bipartisan Campaign Reform Act, Public Law 107-155, 107th Cong., 2nd Sess., section 319, 2 U.S.C. sections 441a-1, 116 Stat. 109, governing House campaigns. The similar BCRA provision governing Senate campaigns, section 304, is set forth at 2 U.S.C. 441a(i), 116 Stat. 97. The "threshold" amount for invoking the amendment against Senate candidates is determined by a complex formula. Both the House and Senate versions of the Millionaire Amendment were rendered void by the Court's ruling.

17. *Davis v. FEC*, 128 S.Ct. 2759 (2008).

18. Ibid. at 2773–74.

19. Corrado and Varney, *Party Money in the 2006 Elections*, 12.

20. David A. Dulio and Candice J. Nelson, *Vital Signs: Perspectives on the Health of American Campaigning*, (Washington, DC: Brookings Institution Press, 2005), 29–30.

21. *FEC v. Wis. Right to Life, Inc.*, 127 S. Ct. 2652 (2007).

Chapter 1: How the Current Campaign Finance System Works For Incumbents and Against Parties

1. Despite such complexities, Trevor Potter, one of the leading proponents of greater campaign finance regulation, holds the view that a certain crucial definition of coordination "depends on the outcome of current and future legal battles." Trevor Potter and Kirk L. Jowers, "Speech Governed by Federal Election Laws," in *The New Campaign Finance Sourcebook*, ed. Anthony Corrado, Thomas E. Mann, Daniel R. Ortiz, and Trevor Potter (Washington, DC: Brookings Institution Press, 2005), 205, 219.

2. 11 C.F.R §§ 109.20–109.37 (2007).

3. *Shays v. FEC*, 528 F.3d 914 (D.C. Cir. 2008).

4. The basic federal statutory scheme is contained in the *Federal Election Campaign Act of 1971*, Public Law 92–225, 92nd Cong., 2nd sess. (February 7, 1972), amended by the *Federal Election Campaign Act Amendments of 1974*, Public Law 93-443, 93rd

Cong., 2nd sess. (October 15, 1974), and the *Bipartisan Campaign Reform Act of 2002* (McCain-Feingold), Public Law 107-155, 107 Cong., 2nd sess. (March 27, 2002). The key regulatory provisions of these laws are codified at 2 U.S.C. §§ 431–57 (2005).

5. See John Samples, *The Fallacy of Campaign Finance Reform* (Chicago: University of Chicago Press, 2006), 168–69; Joel M. Gora, "Campaign Financing and the Nixon Presidency: The End of an Era," in *Richard M. Nixon: Politician, President, Administrator*, ed. Leon Friedman and William F. Levantrosser (New York: Greenwood Press, 1991), 299, 310; and Bradley A. Smith, "Why Campaign Finance Reform Never Works," *Wall Street Journal*, March 19, 1997, A19.

6. Bradley A. Smith, *Unfree Speech: The Folly of Campaign Finance Reform* (Princeton: Princeton University Press, 2001), 36.

7. See Trevor Potter, "The Current State of Campaign Finance Law," in *The New Campaign Finance Sourcebook*, ed. Anthony Corrado, Thomas E. Mann, Daniel R. Ortiz, and Trevor Potter (Washington, DC: Brookings Institution Press, 2005), 48, 76–80; Donald B. Tobin, "Political Advocacy and Taxable Entities: Are They the Next 'Loophole?'" *First Amendment Law Review* 6 (Fall 2007): 41.

8. Robert K. Goidel, Donald August Gross, and Todd G. Shields, *Money Matters: Consequences of Campaign Finance Reform in U.S. House Elections* (Lanham, MD: Rowman & Littlefield, 1999), 23.

9. For this general view see Raymond J. La Raja, *Small Change: Money, Political Parties, and Campaign Finance Reform* (Ann Arbor: University of Michigan Press, 2008).

10. Ibid., 58–63.

11. Johnson's remark is in Lyndon B. Johnson, *Special Message to Congress on Election Reform: The Political Process in America*, 90th Cong., 1st sess., May 25, 1967, http://www.presidency.ucsb.edu/ws/index.php?pid=28268 (accessed October 14, 2008). For the view that these early laws were ineffective, see *Buckley v. Valeo*, 519 F.2d 821, 907 (D.C. Cir. 1975) (noting that laws prior to the FECA were necessary to remedy "the failure of piecemeal regulation to preserve the integrity of federal elections"); see also Bradley A. Smith, *Unfree Speech*, 25–31; Herbert Alexander, *Financing Politics: Money, Elections and Political Reform* (Washington, DC: Congressional Quarterly Press, 1992); and Robert E. Mutch, *Campaigns, Congress, and Courts: The Making of Federal Campaign Finance Law* (New York: Praeger, 1988), 29–32.

12. A well-known book of the era conveyed the theme that political candidates were being marketed to the American people like soap or detergent and that democracy was being sold to the highest bidder. See Joe McGinniss, *The Selling of the President 1968* (New York: Trident Press, 1969).

13. Goidel, Gross, and Shields, *Money Matters*, 34–35.

14. *Political Broadcast Act*, S 3637, 91st Cong., 2nd sess. (1969); President Richard Nixon, Veto of S. 3637, 91st Cong., 2nd sess., *Weekly Compilation of Presidential Documents* (October 19, 1970): 1367–68.

15. Samples, *Fallacy of Campaign Finance Reform*, 199.

16. Cited in ibid., 202. As Samples observes, limiting TV advertising by challengers "was the intention behind the law. Unconstrained spending on television threatened incumbent members of Congress in general and majority control by Democrats in particular." Ibid, 202.

17. See La Raja, *Small Change*, 152, indicating that each of the two major party national committees raised approximately $20 million that year, presumably apart from the mostly autonomous presidential campaigns which raised and spent far more. The Democrats, surprisingly, generally supported the elimination of contribution limits because they thought they would need to rely on a few large contributors to keep the party going in the 1970s. Mutch, *Campaigns, Congress, and Courts*, 66–67.

18. *Federal Election Campaign Act Amendments of 1974*, Pub. L. No. 93-443 (October 15, 1974).

19. See American Civil Liberties Union, *Questions and Answers about Campaign Finances*, pamphlet (New York: 1975)

20. Samples, *Fallacy of Campaign Finance Reform*, 220–22.

21. The public financing benefit, seemingly a positive development, came with a series of severe spending and other restrictions that have caused presidential candidates today largely to abandon the system, which no longer provides sufficient funds for an effective campaign. In addition, the funding scheme was stacked against minor parties or independent candidates—usually stalwart opponents of the status quo—making it extremely difficult for them to qualify for any of the public funds.

22. 424 U.S. 1 (1976).

23. See Special Commission on Campaign Finance Reform, Association of the Bar of the City of New York, *Dollars and Democracy: A Blueprint for Campaign Finance Reform* (New York: Fordham University Press, 2000), 33–34. The Court also invalidated the composition of the FEC because—like the chicken coop guarded by the fox—it was dominated by the leaders of the House and Senate.

24. Bradley A. Smith, *Unfree Speech*, 36.

25. *Buckley*, 424 U.S. at 31 n.33 (emphasis added). However, since the Court invalidated the various expenditure limits, it did not need to "express any opinion with regard to the alleged invidious discrimination resulting from the full sweep of the legislation as enacted." Ibid.

26. Ibid. at 35 n.40.

27. Ibid. at 58 n.66.

28. *FECA Amendments of 1976*, Pub.L. 94-283 (1976).

29. See Anthony Corrado, "Money and Politics: A History of Federal Campaign Finance Law," in *The New Campaign Finance Sourcebook*, ed. Anthony Corrado, Thomas E. Mann, Daniel R. Ortiz, and Trevor Potter (Washington, DC: Brookings Institution Press, 2005), 27–28. As noted above, the FEC also eased the ability of parties to raise what would come to known as soft money to be spent on state and local grassroots support. So, as one observer put it, "Congress was loosening the restrictions on party spending, while the FEC was loosening the restrictions on party fundraising." Ibid., 32. The era of party soft money was about to begin.

30. In a later case, *Randall v. Sorrell*, 548 U.S. 230, 248 (2006), the Court noted that there is a "lower bound" on contributions. They cannot be set so low that they "harm the electoral process by preventing challengers from mounting effective campaigns against incumbent officeholders."

31. 540 U.S. 93 (2003).

32. In 2007, however, the Court revisited the question of broadcast ads mentioning politicians, particularly ads which urged citizens to tell elected representatives to take a stand on particular pieces of pending legislation. *FEC v. Wis. Right to Life, Inc.*, 127 S. Ct. 2652 (2007) ("*WRTL II*"). Clarifying its 2003 *McConnell* ruling, the Court spelled out that advocacy of such "grass-roots lobbying" by any organization could be prohibited "only if the ad is susceptible of no reasonable interpretation other than as an appeal to vote for or against a specific candidate." Ibid., at 2667. And in making that case-by-case determination of whether the ad constituted the "functional equivalent" of express advocacy, the Court "must give the benefit of any doubt to protecting rather than stifling speech"—must give it "to speech, not censorship." Ibid.

33. See Brief of the Appellants at 95-96, *Buckley v. Valeo* 424 U.S. 1 (1976) (Nos. 75-436, 75-437).

34. See ibid. at 58–59, 94–96. The value of the frank during a two-year period was estimated at $104,000. Ibid. Agreed Finding 36, Appendix II, part A (noting that the budgeted cost for 1974 for the franking privilege was approximately $38 million). As Judge Ralph K. Winter, lead counsel for plaintiffs in the *Buckley* case, has observed, "In 1974, the year in which the limits were passed, over $38 million was spent on the congressional frank—the heaviest use of the frank at that time being near the dates of primary and general elections. In the same year, the total spent by challengers in all primary and general election campaigns was barely over $20 million." Ralph K. Winter, "The History and Theory of *Buckley v. Valeo*," *Journal of Law and Policy* 6 (1997): 102. The Court thought the advantages of incumbency were "axiomatic." *Buckley v. Valeo*, 424 U.S. at 31 n.33. Indeed, when there was a proposal to allow challengers a higher spending limit than incumbents, a key senator intoned that this "would kill the bill." Brief of the Appellants at 99, *Buckley*, 424 U.S. 1 (Nos.75-436, 75-437).

35. Bradley A. Smith, "Why Campaign Finance Reform Never Works," A19.

36. Rodney A. Smith, *Money, Power and Elections: How Campaign Finance Reform Subverts American Democracy* (Baton Rouge: Louisiana State University Press, 2006), 107.

37. See *Randall v. Sorrell*, 548 U.S. 230, 241-42 (2006). That decision reaffirmed *Buckley's* categorical rejection of mandatory campaign expenditure limits and rejected the argument that spending limits were valid because they would spare politicians, especially incumbents, from having to spend so much time raising money, rather than governing. Ibid. at 245. Since the law had placed extremely low ceilings on contributions—thereby guaranteeing that it would take a lot of time for all but the most wealthy candidate to raise funds—the argument that fundraising was time-consuming seemed a bit reminiscent of the argument from the youth who murdered his parents and then threw himself on the mercy of the court because he was an

orphan. The only exception to the rule has been that the Court has upheld restrictions on candidate-partisan expenditures by corporations and labor unions. *McConnell v. FEC*, 540 U.S. 93, 203 (2003); *Austin v. Mich. State Chamber of Commerce*, 494 U.S. 652 (1990).

38. *Buckley v. Valeo*, 424 U.S. 1, 54 (1976).

39. In the 2004 elections, 67 percent of the candidates invoking the higher contribution allowances were incumbents. See Jennifer A. Steen, "Self-Financed Candidates and the Millionaire's Amendment," in *The Election after Reform: Money, Politics and the Bipartisan Campaign Reform Act*, ed. Michael J. Malbin (Lanham, MD: Rowman & Littlefield, 2006), 207–10. It was never invoked against an incumbent.

40. Rodney A. Smith, *Money, Power and Elections*, 109–11.

41. Though a lower federal court upheld this provision, the Supreme Court reversed the decision and ruled that the Millionaire Amendment violated the First Amendment because it constituted impermissible congressional manipulation of the campaign finance rules to achieve impermissible goals, such as leveling the playing field, and to privilege certain forms of campaign speech and organization over others. *Davis v. FEC*, 128 S.Ct. 2759, 2773-74 (2008) (reversing *Davis v. FEC*, 501 F. Supp. 2d 22 (D.D.C. 2007) (three-judge panel)). As indicated above, not only is this decision a strong condemnation of incumbents' manipulative use of campaign finance rules to enhance their status, but it casts a dim light on the so-called trigger or rescue provisions of many public financing schemes, which give participating candidates more funds to counter campaigning by nonparticipating candidates and outside groups.

42. *McConnell v. FEC* 540 U.S. 93, 219 (2003).

43. See Anthony Corrado, "Party Finance in the Wake of BCRA: An Overview," in *The Election after Reform: Money, Politics, and the Bipartisan Campaign Reform Act*, ed. Michael J. Malbin (Lanham, MD: Rowman & Littlefield, 2006), 33.

44. *United States v. Nat'l Comm. for Impeachment*, 469 F.2d 1135 (2d Cir. 1972); *ACLU v. Jennings*, 366 F. Supp. 1041 (D.D.C. 1973), vacated by *Staats v. ACLU*, 422 U.S. 1030 (1975) (ordering dismissal of the case as moot).

45. 18 U.S.C. § 608(e)(1). This section was repealed in 1976, as part of the Federal Election Campaign Act Amendments of 1976. See P.L. 94-283, 90 Stat. 496

46. *Buckley v. Valeo*, 424 U.S.1, 47-48 (1976). Since 1976, the Court has frequently reaffirmed that independent campaign speech cannot be limited when engaged in by the following: groups supporting or opposing a publicly funded candidate—see *FEC v. Nat'l Conservative PAC*, 470 U.S. 238 (1986); ideological corporations—see *FEC v. Mass. Citizens for Life*, 479 U.S. 238 (1986); and political parties independently supporting their own candidate or criticizing the opposing candidate—see *Colorado Republican Fed. Campaign Comm. v. FEC*, 518 U.S. 604 (1996) ("*Colorado Republican I*").

47. See Bradley A. Smith, "Faulty Assumptions and Undemocratic Consequences of Campaign Finance Reform," *Yale Law Journal* 105 (January 1996): 1073. Eugene McCarthy's campaign was the paradigm of how challengers and other opponents of the status quo more typically may rely on a small number of large contributors. Ibid. The

arrival of the Internet, however, may have undercut somewhat the antichange aspects of contribution limits by making it easier for a large group of small contributors to have an impact on candidacies, as the experiences of both Senator Barack Obama and Representative Ron Paul have demonstrated.

48. *Randall v. Sorrell*, 548 U.S. 230, 249 (2006).

49. *State Limits on Contributions to Candidates*, National Conference of State Legislatures, August 20, 2008, http://www.ncsl.org/print/legismgt/limits_candidates.pdf (accessed October 15, 2008).

50. See David M. Primo and Jeffrey Milyo, "Campaign Finance Laws and Political Efficacy: The Evidence from the States," *Election Law Journal* 5, no. 1 (2006): 34–36, suggesting no negative impact on government functioning or attitudes about government in states with limited campaign finance controls.

51. See Pew Center on the States, Government Performance Project, "Measuring Performance: The State Management Report Card for 2008," *Governing* (March 2008), http://www.pewcenteronthestates.org/uploadedFiles/Grading-the-States-2008.pdf (accessed October 15, 2008); see also Michael Schrimpf, "Money Well Spent?" Center for Competitive Politics blog, March 7, 2008, at http://www.campaignfreedom.org/blog/ID.530/blog_detail.asp (accessed October 15, 2008).

52. Campaign Finance Institute, *Vital Statistics on Congress 2008*, "Table 3-1: The Cost of Winning an Election, 1986–2006," http://www.cfinst.org/data/pdf/VitalStats_t1.pdf (accessed February 3, 2009).

53. Senator Robert Bennett and Marc Elias (partner, Perkins Coie LLP), colloquy, Senate Committee on Rules and Administration, *Repealing the Limitation on Party Expenditures on Behalf of Candidates in General Elections* [S 1091], 110th Cong., 1st sess., April 18, 2007, http://rules.senate.gov/hearings/2007/041807correctedTranscript.pdf (accessed September 18, 2008).

54. 518 U.S. 604 (1996).

55. *FEC v. Colo. Republican Fed. Campaign Comm.*, 533 U.S. 431 (2001); compare *Colorado Republican I*, 518 U.S. at 604, invalidating limits on a party's independent spending for its candidates.

56. See dissenting opinion of Justice Anthony Kennedy in *Nixon v. Shrink Mo. Gov't PAC*, 528 U.S. 377, 408 (2000) (Kennedy, J., dissenting).

57. In Senate floor debates on the measure, senators characterized these ads as "crack cocaine," "drive-by shootings," "air pollution," "negative ads," "attack ads," "brutal," "a nightmare," and "poison politics." By enacting the bill, the senators were told, they would make such ads largely disappear. *McConnell v. FEC*, 540 U.S. 93, 260 (2003)(Scalia, J., concurring in part and dissenting in part). Justice Scalia also noted many other transparently pro-incumbent features of the BCRA, such as the Millionaire Amendment. Ibid. at 249.

58. *McConnell*, 540 U.S. at 206.

59. 540 U.S. at 248 (Scalia, J. dissenting in part). One other key pending issue about independent spending also has a big impact on incumbents. Under the law, one

individual has the right to spend as much as he wants criticizing or supporting a political candidate during an election—say, for example, $50,000. But what if two such individuals band together? Can they pool their resources and spend $100,000 criticizing that politician, or, by joining together, have they become a political committee which can accept no more than $5,000 from any one person? Put another way, do they have to give up their right of free speech in order to exercise their right to associate? A small group of such individuals, who want to pool their resources to oppose incumbent politicians who favor limits on campaign funding, have gone to court to establish their right to band together, and this may be a landmark case in the battle between free speech and the power of incumbency. In the new math of campaign finance rules, does $1 + 1 = 2$, or does $1 + 1 = 0$? See *SpeechNow.org v. FEC*, 567 F. Supp. 2d 70 (D.D.C. 2008) (holding that such a group of individuals can be limited as a political committee).

One other point is pertinent here. The 2007 Supreme Court ruling in *FEC v. Wisconsin Right to Life, Inc.*, 127 S.Ct. 2652 (2007) [*WRTL II*], which broadened the right of corporations and unions to use soft money to broadcast "electioneering communications" that fall short of being the functional equivalent of express advocacy, is good for free speech and the ability to criticize incumbents. But, relatively speaking, it comes at the expense of candidates and national parties, who are allowed to use only hard money to respond to such attacks, yet another weakening of the status and role of parties affected by our campaign finance rules.

60. *WRTL II*, 127 S. Ct. at 2659.

61. Ibid. at 2667.

62. Ibid. at 2674.

63. As Chief Justice Burger so sensibly noted: "Rank-and-file union members or rising junior executives may now think twice before making even modest contributions to a candidate who is disfavored by the union or management hierarchy. Similarly, potential contributors may well decline to take the obvious risks entailed in making a reportable contribution to the opponent of a well entrenched incumbent." *Buckley v. Valeo*, 424 U.S. 1, 237 (1976) (Burger, C.J., dissenting). A modern version of this same concern was reported in a recent news article about an overly aggressive state attorney general whom people feared to be identified as opposing: for the challenger, "a big hurdle is fund raising, even among a business community that is desperate to throw out [the incumbent]." Potential donors have told him that "I sure hope you beat him, but I can't afford to have my name on your records. He might come after me next." The article calls this case "a frightening example of how the power of an attorney general can corrupt even the electoral process." Kimberley A. Strassel, "Challenging Spitzerism at the Polls," *Wall Street Journal*, August 1, 2008.

64. In *FEC v. Massachusetts Citizens for Life*, 479 U.S. 238, 266 (1986), several justices noted that the difficulties of complying with complex registration, reporting, and disclosure requirements for modestly funded groups may discourage such organizations from engaging in political speech.

65. 2 U.S.C. § 441b(a).

66. In passing the FECA in 1971, Congress specifically added a provision, Section 205, which made it explicit that corporations and unions could set up a "segregated fund," i.e., a PAC, that could receive contributions from its members or employees and could make contributions and expenditures to or on behalf of candidates. See *Pipefitters Local Union v. United States*, 407 U.S. 385, 409-10 (1972). In the years following *Buckley* and its upholding of the $1,000 cap on individual campaign contributions, PACs flourished because of their ability to contribute five times that amount to candidates. One of the major campaign finance "reform" planks of the 1980s was the effort to reduce or eliminate PACS, but with incumbents profiting from them so handsomely, these efforts did not go very far.

67. See Brody Mullins, "Labor Makes a Big Comeback in '08 Races," *Wall Street Journal*, January 18, 2008, noting that labor spent $561 million on political activity in the 2004 and 2006 election cycles, 50 percent more than the $381 million spent in the previous two election years. The *New York Times* recently reported that a coalition of liberal groups was planning to coordinate $350 million in voter mobilization and candidate advocacy efforts, with the AFL-CIO and its affiliate unions kicking in approximately $200 million of that. Michael Luo, "A United Liberal Front," *New York Times*, March 18, 2008.

68. See La Raja, *Small Change*, 80.

69. See Stephen R. Weissman and Ruth Hassan, "BCRA and 527 Groups," in *The Election after Reform: Money, Politics and the Bipartisan Campaign Reform Act*, ed. Michael J. Malbin (Lanham: Rowman & Littlefield, 2006), 79–85; see also Joseph E. Cantor, Erica Lunder, and L. Paige Whitaker, "Congressional Research Service Report for Congress: Section 527 Political Organizations," Report RL33888, February 21, 2007, suggesting that presidential 527s spent $596 million.

70. In the recent right-to-life committee case, Justice Scalia wryly observed the "wondrous irony" "in the fact that the effect of BCRA has been to concentrate more political power in the hands of the country's wealthiest individuals and their so-called 527 organizations, unregulated by [BCRA]. (In the 2004 election cycle, a mere 24 individuals contributed an astounding total of $142 million to 527s.) . . . While these wealthy individuals dominate political discourse, it is this small, grass-roots organization of Wisconsin Right to Life that is muzzled." *WRTL II*, 127 S. Ct. 2652, 2686-87 (2007) (internal citation omitted).

71. Nonprofit organizations can receive unlimited donations for voter identification and get-out-the-vote activities, and such organizations already receive large donations, sometimes in the millions of dollars, for these activities. For example, the NAACP Voter Fund received a single, anonymous $7 million donation for get-out-the-vote activities in connection with the 2000 elections. *McConnell v. FEC*, 540 U.S. 93, 176 n.68 (2003). That was the same election where the NAACP ran television ads seeking to hold then-governor George Bush responsible for the lynching of a black man, James Byrd. Again in 2004, the partisan anti-Bush speeches of NAACP chairman Julian Bond led to an IRS investigation for improper political intervention by a 501(c)(3) organization. Elizabeth

Wasserman, "Nonprofits Walk Fine Line on Political Activity," MSNBC, July 28, 2008, http://www.msnbc.msn.com/id/25838144/ (accessed October 15, 2008), notes that the IRS cited seventy-five charities, including many churches, for engaging in prohibited political activities during the 2004 presidential election, and three charities had their tax-exempt status revoked.

72. Jonathan D. Salant, "Obama Leveraged Record Fundraising, Spending to Defeat Rivals," Bloomberg.com, November 5, 2008, http://www.bloomberg.com/appsnews?pid=20601087&sid=axZ6QT0Qr3YQ&refer=worldwide (accessed January 30, 2009).

73. See, e.g., *Davis v. FEC*, 128 S.Ct. 2759, 2771-74 (2008) (calling in serious question the validity of such triggering mechanisms); but see *Green Party of Conn. v. Garfield*, 537 F. Supp. 2d 359 (D. Conn. 2008) (finding that trigger provisions "do not actually burden the exercise of political speech").

74. *Fair Elections Now Act*, S. 936, 110th Cong. § 511 (2007) (providing for payment of "fair fight funds").

Chapter 2: Other Reforms: Would They Make Things Better or Worse?

1. "Has the U.S. Campaign Finance System Collapsed?" *Forum* 6, no. 1 (March 2008), http://www.bepress.com/forum/vol6/iss1/ (accessed October 15, 2008).

2. "Study after study shows that contributions play little or no role in how politicians vote. One of the most comprehensive, conducted by a group of MIT scholars in 2004, concluded that 'indicators of party, ideology and district preferences account for most of the systematic variation in legislators' roll call voting behavior.'" Bradley A. Smith, "The Speech Police," *Wall Street Journal*, June 27, 2007. The MIT study is Stephen Ansolabehere, John M. deFigueiredo, and James M. Snyder, Jr., "Why Is There So Little Money in U.S. Politics?" *Journal of Economic Perspectives* 17 (2003). See also John Samples, *The Fallacy of Campaign Finance Reform* (Chicago: University of Chicago Press, 2006), 88–100; and Stephen G. Bronars and John R. Lott, Jr., "Do Campaign Donations Alter How a Politician Votes?" *Journal of Law and Economics* 40 (October 1997): 317–50, demonstrating that legislators who had announced their retirement from office, when contributions no longer matter to them, voted the same way they did before.

3. See *Nixon v. Shrink Mo. Gov't PAC*, 528 U.S. 377, 408 (2000) (Kennedy, J., dissenting).

4. See *Shays v. FEC*, 511 F. Supp. 2d 19 (D.D.C. 2007) (criticizing the FEC's failure to develop a regulation for deciding when to treat 527s as political committees but upholding the commission's prerogative to continue to determine FECA coverage on a case-by-case basis in deciding whether a 527's "major purpose" is partisan), rev'd in part, 528 F.3d 914 (D.C. Cir. 2008); see generally Paul S. Ryan, "527s in 2008: The Past, Present and Future of 527 Organization Political Activity Regulation," *Harvard Journal of Legislation* 45 (Summer 2008): 471–506.

5. The enforcement matters are collected in a recent court decision, *SpeechNow.Org v. FEC*, 567 F.Supp.2d 70 (D.D.C. 2008); see also "FEC to Collect $750,000 Civil Penalty from Progress for America Voter Fund," *State News Service*, February 28, 2007.

6. *SpeechNow.Org v. FEC*, 567 F.Supp.2d 70 (D.D.C. 2008) (refusing to enjoin FEC rules that treated two individuals as a political committee, noting the need to enforce FECA rules more aggressively against 527s that try to influence federal elections yet steer clear of FECA controls). At the same time, another court upheld more stringent FECA regulation of 527s that solicit contributions by indicating they will be used to support or oppose candidates. See *Emily's List v. FEC*, 569 F. Supp.2d 18 (D.D.C. 2008).

7. Leslie Wayne, "Clinton Aide's Private Databank Venture Breaks Ground in Politicking," *New York Times*, April 12, 2008. The company, Catalist, was created by Harold Ickes, a long-time associate of the Clintons. It seemed to emerge from the remnants of the various pro-Democratic 527 groups active during the 2004 elections, and had received start-up "investment" funds from the usual liberal fat cats, with George Soros topping the list. The concern is that in providing voter mobilization services and information to liberal candidates and groups, Catalist will use a business format to mask political activities and avoid accountability: "But some campaign finance watchdogs say they wonder whether Catalist was established not so much to make money but to find a creative way to allow big-money liberal donors to influence the election without disclosing the degree of their involvement or being subjected to other rules that would govern spending by an explicitly political organization." Ibid.

8. As Bradley A. Smith has pointed out, what is called "public financing" is really a euphemism for government financing. Truly public financing comes from the millions of members of the public who contribute their own funds to the candidates or parties of their choice. Bradley A. Smith, *Unfree Speech: The Folly of Campaign Finance Reform* (Princeton: Princeton University Press, 2001), 88. President Barack Obama, the reformer who abandoned his commitment to government financing and relied entirely on private financing for his primary and general election campaigns, adopted Professor Smith's theory to justify his rejection of public financing, namely, that he had developed a "parallel public financing system" and that his campaign was being financed by "the public." Jake Tapper, "Obama Prepares Argument to Discard Public-Financing Principle," ABC News Online, April 8, 2008, http://blogs.abcnews.com/politicalpunch/2008/04/obama-prepares.html (accessed October 15, 2008).

9. See New York City Campaign Finance Board, *Public Dollars for the Public Good: A Report on the 2005 Elections* (New York: New York City Campaign Finance Board, 2006), 37, 2, http://www.nyccfb.info/PDF/per/2005_PER/2005_Post_Election_Report.pdf (accessed October 15, 2008). Ironically, in the face of the failure of generous government subsidies to increase electoral competition or benefit challengers over incumbents, that board recommended that the matching funds—at that point at an extremely high level of 4 to 1—be increased further to 5 to 1 or even 6 to 1, which was thereafter enacted. Ibid., 9. Despite that fact, and though the number of small contributors to citywide electoral campaigns has recently increased, the overall fundraising level has declined.

See Abraham Riesman, "Number of Small Campaign Contributors Soars," *New York Sun*, July 25, 2008. Rather than fostering competition, public funding and term limits can create "a political revolving door" where outgoing incumbents seek other elective office and, in turn, are replaced by family members or former staffers, thereby making insurgency "virtually impossible." Diane Cardwell, "Here They Run Again: Term Limits Don't Seem to Faze Council Members," *New York Times*, June 9, 2008. So much for competition. As to serving as an antidote to corruption, the New York City public funding experience falls short there as well: in 2008, Council Speaker Christine C. Quinn disclosed that, since at least 2001, members of the New York City Council appropriated millions in taxpayer dollars for fictitious groups, which allowed them to spend the money later on favored community programs without obtaining the mayor's approval. According to Ms. Quinn, the practice encompassed the tenures of the previous two speakers, Peter F. Vallone, Sr., and Gifford Miller. Ray Rivera and Russ Beuttner, "Speaker Says Council Allotted Cash to Fake Groups and Spent It Elsewhere," *New York Times*, April 4, 2008. As even the *New York Times* was forced to admit editorially, these slush funds "are, at best, a political trick intended to buy voter loyalty. At worst, they have led to outright theft." *New York Times*, "New York's Slush Addiction," April 29, 2008. It seems as if some of these politicians were running their own private, off-the-books public financing program. High-priced lawyers have been hired, at public expense of course, to defend these politicians in criminal investigations. So much for public financing as the antidote to corruption.

10. See *Green Party of Conn. v. Garfield*, 537 F. Supp. 2d 359, 385-92 (D. Conn. 2008) (discussing various state public funding schemes).

11. See *Fair Elections Now Act*, S. 1285, 110th Cong., 1st sess. (2007). There have long been proposals to provide for free television or radio broadcast time to political candidates, while other approaches would provide candidates with vouchers to purchase advertisements in several kinds of media outlets. Though these schemes have serious flaws in them (as we indicate later in this chapter), they at least generally attempt to expand political communication and opportunity, though many of them also involve strings such as agreeing to limit overall spending, and, in some cases, agreeing not to use the free time to attack one's opponents.

12. See Richard L. Hasen, "Clipping Coupons for Democracy: An Egalitarian/Public Choice Defense of Campaign Finance Vouchers," *California Law Review* 84 (January 1996): 1–59; Edward B. Foley, "Equal-Dollars-Per-Voter: A Constitutional Principle of Campaign Finance," *Columbia Law Review* 94 (1994): 1204–57.

13. See C. Edwin Baker, "Reclaiming the First Amendment: Constitutional Theories of Media Reform: The Independent Significance of the Press Clause under Existing Law," *Hofstra Law Review* 35 (Spring 2007): 993–95.

14. Joel Gora, "Book Review: 'No Law . . . Abridging,'" *Harvard Journal of Law & Public Policy* 24 (Summer 2001): 871.

15. There was indeed a brief time, beginning in 1971, when you could take a modest $100 deduction or receive a $50 credit on your federal joint tax return for a

contribution to a federal or state or local political candidate. See *Revenue Act of 1971*, Public Law 92-178, 92nd Cong., 1st sess. (1971). In 1974, Congress increased the deduction and credit. Four years later, Congress increased the credit again but repealed the deduction, citing the need to simplify tax forms. House Ways and Means Committee, *Revenue Act of 1978*, HR 1445, 95th Cong., 2nd sess., Pub. L. 95-600 (1978). The credit was repealed a few years later, also as part of tax simplification. Public Law 99-514. This does not seem like a legitimate reason for eliminating an excellent program.

16. One could make some provision for those registered voters who do not file income taxes or do not itemize their deductions in a given year by providing them with a voucher or coupon that could be donated to the candidate or party of their choice. See Bruce Ackerman and Ian Ayres, "Fixing the System That Obama Broke," *American Prospect*, July 3, 2008, http://www.prospect.org/cs/articles?article=fixing__the_system_obama_broke (accessed October 15, 2008). But, of course, adding this wrinkle to a tax-based system would undercut the next goal of a promising program, namely, ease of administration. We disagree with Ackerman and Ayres's overall proposal for so-called patriot dollars because it would coerce candidates into financing their campaigns only with such resources, but we would observe that those scholars share our view about the stifling defects of the current system: "Current law tries to limit big money by restricting the flow of private funds into politics. But this restrictionist approach generates two problems. It inevitably reduces the amount of political debate—less money means less speech. And it distorts the balance of power between incumbents and challengers. Officeholders have public reputations generated by high visibility, and challengers need lots of cash to offset this advantage. So drastic restrictions on private funds allow incumbents to tighten their grip on power under the banner of reform." Ibid.

17. There was a time when some states provided public funding for candidates without expenditure limits, i.e., they provided floors without ceilings. Massachusetts and Montana were two such states. See Herbert Alexander, *Financing Politics: Money, Elections and Political Reform* (Washington, DC: Congressional Quarterly Press, 1992), 130–31. Today, most public financing schemes require participants to agree "voluntarily" to spending limits. But an influential United States senator, Bob Graham of Florida, has argued persuasively that public funding would achieve more without such limits. Endorsing that approach, the well-regarded campaign finance lawyer Robert Bauer has argued thus:

> Do away with limits altogether. There is really no way to set them with any precision. And if the candidate can escape limits in any one case—where an opponent does not abide by them—then the proposals now on the table concede that a public funding alternative without limits is conceivable.
>
> Relieved by the burden of overall (or state-by-state) spending limits, candidates would still have to raise their private money within limits, contribution by contribution. Their success or failure as candidates will determine how much of this limited money they can raise. They should be able to spend what

they raise and not be stifled by limits artificially set and shown, by experience, to be beyond the government's capacity to define with much success.

Public money might get a candidate started, when getting started is the principal problem, and that is a good thing. Then it would be up to the candidate to raise what can be raised and to spend all that can be spent.

See Robert Bauer, "Presidential Public Financing Reform and the Problem of Spending Limits," *More Soft Money Hard Law*, January 30, 2008, http://www.moresoftmoneyhard law.com/moresoftmoneyhardlaw/updates/other_related_legal_developments.html?AID =1184 (accessed October 15, 2008).

18. The scholar proposing this option was Daniel Hays Lowenstein; see his "On Campaign Finance Reform: The Root of All Evil Is Deeply Rooted," *Hofstra Law Review* 18 (1989): 348–64; see also Alexander, *Financing Politics*, 126–44. Note also that many European countries give various forms of subsidies directly to parties.

19. The FEC planned to increase the overall sum available to the parties' presidential nominating conventions in 2008 to include a "cost of living adjustment" for that year. Federal Election Commission, "Press Release: Both Major Parties to Receive Public Funding for 2008 Conventions," June 26, 2007, http://www.fec.gov/press/press2007/20070626conventions. shtml (accessed October 15, 2008).

20. *Buckley v. Valeo*, 424 U.S. 1, 292 (1976)(Rehnquist, J., concurring in part and dissenting in part). Just recently, for example, a federal judge condemned Connecticut's new public financing scheme as favoring the two major parties over minor and insurgent parties and candidates. *Green Party of Conn. v. Garfield*, 537 F. Supp. 2d 359, 385-92 (D. Conn. 2008). In the initial stages of serious consideration of public financing of campaigns, there were proposals that would have provided funding directly to political parties, without use of a taxpayer check-off mechanism. See Robert E. Mutch, *Campaigns, Congress, and Courts: The Making of Federal Campaign Finance Law* (New York: Praeger, 1988), 37.

21. Although some courts have upheld such trigger mechanisms against constitutional challenge, see *N. C. Right to Life Comm. Fund v. Leake*, 524 F.3d 427 (4th Cir. 2008); *Green Party of Conn. v. Garfield*, 537 F. Supp. 2d at 385-92, their tendency to force candidates into the limitations of the public financing system seems obvious. The Supreme Court's clear concern that campaign finance systems not be rigged to make it difficult to run an effective campaign would seem to undercut this kind of approach. See *Randall v. Sorrell*, 548 U.S. 230, 238-39 (2006). And the Court's recent decision throwing out the Millionaire Amendment's triggering mechanism, which raised the contribution cap to protect "participating candidates," as improper congressional stacking of the electoral deck would seem to have an even more ominous implication for public financing triggers. See *Davis v. FEC*, 128 S. Ct. 2759 (2008). Floor debate on that flawed provision clearly revealed that it was sold to incumbents as a device to protect them from reelection challenge by a significant self-financed candidate. See Brief for Gene DeRossett and J. Edgar Broyhill II as Amici Curiae in Support of Appellant at 12, 22, *Davis v. FEC*, 128 S. Ct. 2759 (2008)(No. 07-320).

22. See *Buckley v. Valeo*, 424 U.S. 1, 292 (1976), upholding the key features of the Presidential Election Campaign Fund; and *Federal Election Campaign Act Amendments of 1974*, Pub. L. 93-443, amending Subtitle H, of the Internal Revenue Code (1974) (codified at 26 U.S.C. § 9001, et seq).

23. To the extent that soft money, despite the public financing system, became a dominant feature of presidential elections, the post-BCRA migration of that money from political parties to 527, 501(c)(3), and 501(c)(4) groups has resulted in much less transparency and accountability compared to the days when parties were utilizing it. Though contributions to 527 groups are subject to reporting, the disclosure comes through the IRS, not the FEC, and seems much less practically accessible. More significantly, a lot of the former party soft money migrated to 501(c)(4)s in 2004, and such funding is protected against public disclosure by IRS rules governing nonprofit organizations. As one recent article noted, once 527 groups had some obligation to report, "more and more groups began to form under section 501(c)(4)—groups like MoveOn.Org on the left and the Employee Freedom Action Committee on the right." Joseph Gerth, "Ad Funding Should Have to Be Revealed," *Louisville Courier Journal*, August 11, 2008.

24. Alexander's book on the 1976 election, *Financing the 1976 Election* (Washington, DC: Congressional Quarterly Press, 1979), recognized the tremendous impact of the public financing system on the ability of candidates to compete. That system ended the era when a candidate would gather ten contributors for a million-dollar fundraiser, and thus brought a well-known candidate like Senator Henry Jackson (D-Wash.), who could probably have done that sort of thing, down to the level of a little-known candidate like Jimmy Carter, who could not. Carter needed federal subsidies to consolidate his initial lead and otherwise could have been swamped by better-known candidates who had connections with wealthy contributors. See Fred Barbash, "Public Election Financing Seen Cutting Grass Roots," *Washington Post*, September 9, 1979, A8. Or, as John Samples put it: "The presidential funding system probably threw the 1976 election to the Democratic candidate, Jimmy Carter." Samples, *Fallacy of Campaign Finance Reform*, 232.

25. Ibid., 202–4. It is difficult to think of any valid purpose to sustain the state-by-state limits on spending for those who accept presidential primary matching funds, except to prejudice certain regionally attractive candidacies, such as Eugene J. McCarthy or Senator John Edwards. All of this becomes particularly suspect in light of the Court's insistence in *Davis v. FEC* that campaign finance restrictions cannot be used to manipulate the electoral process in ways that favor certain types of candidates and methods of campaigning over others. 128 S. Ct. 2759, 2773 (2008). .

26. Though candidates are permitted to accept contributions to defray legal and accounting costs, and voters can make a contribution to the candidate's party, neither of those secondary methods of expressing support can substitute for making a contribution to support the candidate's message. See *Republican Nat'l Comm. v. FEC*, 487 F. Supp. 280 (S.D.N.Y. 1980), aff'd, 445 U.S. 945 (1980).

27. Among the supporters of this effort is a group called "Just $6."

28. The Congressional Research Service puts the number at sixteen in a 2007 report, noting the difference between its definition of "public financing" and the definition used by some private campaign finance reform groups that put the number higher. Joseph E. Cantor and R. Sam Garrett, *Congressional Research Service Report for Congress: Public Financing of Congressional Elections*, Report RL33814, January 22, 2007, 37. Obviously, groups pushing for this mechanism want to create a sense of its prevalence.

29. Jon Wildermuth, "The 'Clean' Campaign Finance Idea Grows," *San Francisco Chronicle*, September 18, 2006; see also Stephen M. Hoersting, testimony, Senate Committee on Rules and Administration, *S. 1285, The Fair Elections Now Act: To Reform the Finance of Senate Elections* and *On the High Cost of Broadcasting Campaign Advertisements*, 110th Cong., 1st sess., June 20, 2007, 9–10, http://rules.senate.gov/hearings/2007/062007Hoersting.pdf (accessed October 15, 2008).

30. Indeed, as part of the McCain-Feingold bill, Congress stipulated that the Government Accounting Office study both systems to see if they would provide good models for the future. See General Accounting Office, "Campaign Finance Reform: Early Experiences of Two States That Offer Full Public Funding for Political Candidates," GAO-03-453, May 2003, 1. That report wound up finding very little positive in the two experiments, and a privately researched report on citizens' confidence in government concluded that the program was unsuccessful. See David M. Primo and Jeffrey Milyo, "Campaign Finance Laws and Political Efficacy: The Evidence from the States," *Election Law Journal* 5, no. 1 (March 2006): 34–36, http://www.liebertonline.com/doi/pdfplus/10.1089/elj.2006.5.23. Other studies have reached a similarly negative conclusion about first-generation programs: "There is no evidence to support the claim that programs combining public funding with spending limits have leveled the playing field, countered the effects of incumbency and made elections more competitive." Michael M. Malbin and Thomas L. Gais, *The Day after Reform: Sobering Campaign Finance Lessons from the American States* (Albany: Rockefeller Institute Press, 1998), 137.

31. See Hoersting, Senate Committee, *Fair Elections Now*, 9; see also Patrick Basham and Martin Zelder, "Does Cleanliness Lead to Competitiveness? The Failure of Maine's Experiment," in *Welfare for Politicians? Taxpayer Financing of Campaigns*, ed. John Samples (Washington, DC: Cato Institute, 2005), 102–3.

32. Hoersting, Senate Committee, *Fair Elections Now*, 9–12. The Democratic candidate benefited from enormous labor union spending, which was not of course matched, while funds raised privately by the Republican opponent were matched by government subsidies for the Democratic opponent in an almost punitive way. Thus, for example, when the Republicans raised $750,000 at an event attended by President Bush, but cleared only $500,000 after expenses, the Democratic "clean" candidate was given a countering grant of the full $750,000. Ibid., 10. It does not take too many election cycles like that to drive home the message and drive the candidates into the "clean election" system.

33. John Samples reports that the typical decline in the participation in state checkoff schemes went from 20 percent to 11 percent in the two decades from 1975 to 1994. Samples, *Fallacy of Campaign Finance Reform*, 185.

34. As Senator Mitch McConnell put it: "There's a growing movement within the States to reverse taxpayer-funded elections at the state level. Just last year my own state of Kentucky eliminated the practice." Senate Committee on Rules and Administration, *S. 1285, The Fair Elections Now Act: To Reform the Finance of Senate Elections* and *On the High Cost of Broadcasting Campaign Advertisements,* 110th Cong., 1st sess., June 20, 2007, 10, http://rules.senate.gov/hearings/2007/062007correctedTranscript.pdf (accessed October 15, 2008).

35. Hoersting, Senate Committee, *Fair Elections Now*, 1.

36. *Fair Elections Now Act,* S. 1285, 110th Cong., 1st sess. §§ 504–6, 511 (2007).

37. See *Buckley v. Valeo,* 424 U.S. 1, 292 (1976); see also *Randall v. Sorrell,* 548 U.S. 230, 238-39 (2006). Also typical of the slanted approach is that in one of the bills, individuals could get up to a $500 tax credit for making a contribution to the fund out of which "clean" candidates would be subsidized, but there is no comparable credit for a contribution to a privately financed candidate. *Fair Elections Now Act,* S. 936, 110th Cong., 1st sess. §112 (2007). Other benefits such as broadcast discounts seem also to be available only to participating candidates and not to nonparticipating ones; this discrepancy constitutes yet another form of pressure to coerce candidates into the system and the limits that obtain. Ibid.; and *Fair Elections Now Act,* S. 1285, 110th Cong., 1st sess. (2007).

38. New York City Campaign Finance Board, *The Impact of High-Spending Non-Participants on the Campaign Finance Program* (New York: New York City Campaign Finance Board, 2006), 3.

39. Center for Competitive Politics, "Overview of Government-Financed Elections" (June 20, 2007), 1, http://www.campaignfreedom.org/docLib/20070720_Glossy.pdf (accessed October 15, 2008).

40. *Wall Street Journal,* "Clinton Foundation Secrets," April 25, 2008.

41. See Bradley A. Smith, "The Speech Police"; see also Stephen Ansolabehere, John M. deFigueiredo, and James M. Snyder, Jr., "Why Is There So Little Money in U.S. Politics?"; Stephen G. Bronars and John R. Lott, Jr., "Do Campaign Donations Alter How a Politician Votes?"; and John Samples, *The Fallacy of Campaign Finance Reform.*

42. *CBS, Inc. v. FCC,* 453 U.S. 367 (1981).

43. One active group was known as the Free TV for Straight Talk Coalition. A particularly trenchant criticism of these proposals can be found in Lillian R. BeVier, *Is Free TV for Federal Candidates Constitutional?* (Washington, DC: AEI Press, 1998).

44. For more on this point, see ibid.

45. Bruce Ackerman and Ian Ayres, *Voting with Dollars: A New Paradigm for Campaign Finance* (New Haven: Yale University Press, 2002).

46. The two primary proponents of this theory are professors Richard Hasen and Edward Foley. See Richard Hasen, "Campaign Finance Laws and the Rupert Murdoch Problem," *Texas Law Review* 77 (1999): 1627–65; and Hasen, "Clipping Coupons for Democracy"; see also Foley, "Equal-Dollars-Per-Voter."

47. See Ackerman and Ayres, *Voting with Dollars,* 93–110.

Chapter 3: The Benefits of Lifting Campaign Finance
Restrictions on Parties

1. Marjorie Randon Hershey, *Party Politics in America*, 11th ed. (New York: Pearson Longman, 2005), 29.

2. A full description of the advantages of incumbency and incumbents appears in James C. Miller III, *Monopoly Politics* (Stanford, CA: Hoover Institution Press, 1999), 75–101.

3. Robert K. Goidel, Donald A. Gross, and Todd G. Shields, *Money Matters: Consequences of Campaign Finance Reform in U.S. House Elections* (Lanham, MD: Rowman & Littlefield, 1999), 62–63.

4. Ibid., 109–11.

5. Campaign Finance Institute, "Table 3-3: Expenditures of House Incumbents and Challengers, by Election Outcome, 1974–2008 (mean net dollars)," forthcoming, http://www.cfinst.org/. Data provided to authors by Campaign Finance Institute executive director Michael Malbin in February 2009.

6. Rodney A. Smith, *Money, Power and Elections: How Campaign Finance Reform Subverts American Democracy* (Baton Rouge: Louisiana State University Press, 2006), 109–14.

7. Campaign Finance Institute, "Table 3-6: Expenditures of Senate Incumbents and Challengers, by Election Outcome, 1980–2008 (mean net dollars)," forthcoming, http://www.cfinst.org/. Data provided to authors by Campaign Finance Institute executive director Michael Malbin in February 2009. The numbers for 2008 where incumbents won with less than 60 percent of the vote are approximate because the race in Minnesota had not been decided when this book went to press.

8. Miller, *Monopoly Politics*, 39.

9. Thomas E. Mann and Norman J. Ornstein, *The Broken Branch: How Congress Is Failing America and How to Get It Back on Track* (New York: Oxford University Press, 2006), 229.

10. See *FEC v. Colo. Republican Fed. Campaign Comm.*, 533 U.S. 431 (2001).

11. Ibid.

12. *Davis v. FEC*, 128 S. Ct. 2759, 2791 (2008).

13. Anthony Corrado, "Party Finance in the Wake of BCRA: An Overview," in *The Election after Reform: Money, Politics, and the Bipartisan Campaign Reform Act*, ed. Michael J. Malbin (Lanham, MD: Rowman & Littlefield, 2006), 22–24.

14. The Center for Responsive Politics notes that Obama raised $745 million for his presidential campaign. See Center for Responsive Politics, "Summary Data for Barack Obama," December 31, 2008, http://www.opensecrets.org/pres08/summary.php?cycle=2008&cid=N00009638 (accessed February 12, 2009). The Campaign Finance Institute reports that "49% of Obama's funds came in discrete contributions of $200 or less" but only "24% of his funds through October 15 . . . came from donors whose total contributions *aggregated* to $200 or less." Campaign Finance Institute, "Reality Check: Obama Received About the Same Percentage from Small Donors in 2008 as Bush in

2004," November 24, 2008, http://www.cfinst.org/pr/prRelease.aspx?ReleaseID=216 (accessed February 12, 2009).

15. John Samples, "An Evaluation of the Campaign Accountability Act of 2007," Senate Committee on Rules and Administration, *Repealing the Limitation on Party Expenditures on Behalf of Candidates in General Elections* [*S 1091*], 110th Cong., 1st sess., April 18, 2007, 5, http://rules.senate.gov/hearings/2007/041807Samples.pdf (accessed September 18, 2008).

16. *FEC v. Colo. Republican Fed. Campaign Comm.*, 533 U.S. 431, 465 (2001) [*Colorado Republican II*].

17. *Colorado Republican II*, 533 U.S. at 475 (Thomas, J., dissenting).

18. John Samples, *The Fallacy of Campaign Finance Reform* (Chicago: University of Chicago Press, 2006), 88.

19. Stephen Ansolabehere, John M. de Figueiredo, and James M. Snyder, Jr., "Why Is There So Little Money in U.S. Politics?" *Journal of Economic Perspectives* 17 (Winter 2003): 116.

20. See, e.g., *United States v. Playboy Entertainment Group*, 529 U.S. 803 (2000) (applying strict scrutiny to strike down congressional regulation of sexual material on cable television).

21. Rodney A. Smith, *Money, Power and Elections*, 118.

22. Ibid., 107.

23. Ibid., 105.

24. Ibid., 8.

25. Center for Responsive Politics, "New Web Tools Track Congressional Finances and Travel," October 10, 2006, http://sunsite.berkeley.edu/govblog/?p=190 (accessed February 12, 2009).

26. Jessica Holzer, "Meet Senator Millionaire," Forbes.com, November 20, 2006, http://www.forbes.com/beltway/2006/11/17/senate-politics-washington-biz-wash_cx_jh_1120senate.html (accessed September 18, 2008).

27. L. Sandy Maisel, "The Incumbency Advantage," in *Money, Elections and Democracy: Reforming Congressional Campaign Finance*, ed. Margaret Latus Nugent and John R. Johannes (Boulder, CO: Westview Press, 1990), 123–24.

28. David A. Dulio and Candice J. Nelson, *Vital Signs: Perspectives on the Health of American Campaigning* (Washington, DC: Brookings Institution Press, 2005), 55.

29. Ibid., 65.

30. Ibid., 92.

31. Cited in Hershey, *Party Politics in America*, 237.

32. 548 U.S. 230 (2006).

33. See, e.g., Ansolabehere, de Figueiredo, and Snyder, "Why Is There So Little Money in U.S. Politics?"

34. Larry J. Sabato and Bruce A. Larson, *The Party's Just Begun: Shaping Political Parties for America's Future*, 2nd ed. (New York: Longman, 2002), 77.

35. Diana Dwyre and Robin Kolodny, "The Parties' Congressional Campaign Committees in 2004," in *The Election after Reform: Money, Politics, and the Bipartisan*

Campaign Reform Act, ed. Michael J. Malbin (Lanham, MD: Rowman & Littlefield, 2006), 51.

36. Dulio and Nelson, *Vital Signs*, 30–31.

37. Samuel L. Popkin, *The Reasoning Voter: Communication and Persuasion in Presidential Campaigns*, 2nd ed. (Chicago: University of Chicago Press, 1994), 212.

38. Carl Ingram, "The State: Davis OKs Redistricting that Keeps Status Quo," *Los Angeles Times*, September 28, 2001, 12.

Chapter 4: The Governance Benefits of Party-Centered Campaign Finance

1. V. O. Key, Jr., *Politics, Parties and Pressure Groups*, 5th ed. (New York: Thomas Y. Crowell, 1969), 9.

2. George Washington, "Farewell Address to Congress," in *Perspectives on Political Parties: Classic Readings*, Susan E. Scarrow, ed. (New York: Palgrave Macmillan, 2002), 48.

3. Nancy L. Rosenblum, "Primus Inter Pares: Political Parties and Civil Society," *Chicago-Kent Law Review* 75, no. 2 (2000): 498.

4. Ibid.

5. Larry J. Sabato and Bruce A. Larson, *The Party's Just Begun: Shaping Political Parties for America's Future*, 2nd ed. (New York: Longman, 2002), 126.

6. Thomas E. Mann and Norman J. Ornstein, *The Broken Branch: How Congress Is Failing America and How to Get It Back on Track* (New York: Oxford University Press, 2006), xi.

7. Ibid., 93.

8. Ibid., 45.

9. Joel H. Silbey, "Foundation Stones of Present Discontents: The American Political Nation, 1776–1945," in *Present Discontents: American Politics in the Very Late Twentieth Century*, ed. Byron Shafer (Chatham, NJ: Chatham House, 1997), 25.

10. David A. Dulio and Candice J. Nelson, *Vital Signs: Perspectives on the Health of American Campaigning* (Washington, DC: Brookings Institution Press, 2005), 27–28.

11. John H. Aldrich, *Why Parties? The Origin and Transformation of Political Parties in America* (Chicago: University of Chicago Press, 1995), 17.

12. Dulio and Nelson, *Vital Signs*, 29.

13. Robert K. Goidel, Donald A. Gross, and Todd G. Shields, *Money Matters: Consequences of Campaign Finance Reform in U.S. House Elections* (Lanham, MD: Rowman & Littlefield, 1999), 4.

14. Aldrich, *Why Parties*, 4.

15. Sabato and Larson, *The Party's Just Begun*, 95–96.

16. Ibid., 112.

17. Aldrich, *Why Parties*, 170.

18. Ibid., 18.

19. Ibid., 9.

20. Cited in American Enterprise Institute, *Political Report* 3, no. 7 (July/August 2007): 6.

21. Mann and Ornstein, *Broken Branch*, 16.

22. Woodrow Wilson, "Responsible Party Government," in *Perspectives on Political Parties: Classic Readings,* ed. Susan E. Scarrow (New York: Palgrave Macmillan, 2002), 163–64.

23. Committee on Political Parties, American Political Science Association, *Toward a More Responsible Two-Party System* (New York: Rinehart & Company, 1950).

24. Ibid., 15.

25. Sabato and Larson, *The Party's Just Begun*, 12. According to Sabato and Larson, "some 69 percent of the specific platform positions were taken by one party but not the other." The study they cite is by Gerald M. Pomper with Susan Lederman, *Elections in America*, 2nd ed. (New York: Longman, 1980), 145–50, 167–73.

26. Sabato and Larson, *The Party's Just Begun*, 15–16.

27. Aldrich, *Why Parties*, 3.

28. American Political Science Association, *Toward a More Responsible Two-Party System*, 19.

29. Sidney M. Milkis, *Political Parties and Constitutional Government: Remaking American Democracy* (Baltimore: Johns Hopkins University Press, 1999), 67.

Conclusion: Now, It's Up to Congress

1. *WRTL II*, 127 S. Ct. 2652, 2686-87 (2007) (Scalia, J., dissenting).

2. See *FEC v. Colo. Republican Fed. Campaign Comm.*, 533 U.S. 431 (2001) [*Colorado Republican II*].

3. Two mechanisms in campaign finance law offer persuasive parallels. First, the Snowe-Jeffords Amendment to the BCRA provided that nonprofit corporations, otherwise barred from making electioneering communications, could nonetheless do so if they set up a separate fund for those broadcasts, accepted contributions only from individuals, and reported contributions in excess of $1,000. See 2 U.S.C. § 441b(c)(2). It was rendered useless by the so-called Wellstone Amendment, which, in effect, cancelled the exemption. See 2 U.S.C. § 441b(c)(6). Similarly, the presidential primary matching funds system matches only the first $250 of individual contributions, in part to recognize the importance of small donations. Here too setting up a special fund for small contributions to be used for permitted coordinated expenditures would serve to encourage participation.

4. Two cases recently filed seek to loosen the current statutory restrictions on party use of hard money and soft money on First Amendment grounds, arguing that coordinated expenditures and soft money should be allowed to support activities that are not unambiguously campaign related or are not the functional equivalent of express

advocacy. Both cases rely on the *WRTLII* ruling which tightened the definitions of the kinds of political activity that could be subject to campaign finance restrictions. See *Cao v. FEC*, No.08-4887 (E.D.La), challenging the scope of the coordinated expenditure limits on some kinds of national party support of its congressional candidates, and *RNC v. FEC*, No. 08-1953 (D.D.C. three-judge court), challenging the restriction on party soft money funding of some kinds of political activity not directly related to campaigns.

5. Byron York, "The Republican Flip-Flop on Campaign-Finance Reform," *National Review Online*, March 30, 2006, http://www.nationalreview.com/york/york2006 03300734.asp (accessed October 15, 2008).

6. Alexander Bolton, "McCain, House GOP Strike a BCRA Deal," *The Hill*, April 6, 2006, 1.

7. See generally Senate Committee on Rules and Administration, *Repealing the Limitation on Party Expenditures on Behalf of Candidates in General Elections* [S 1091], 110th Cong., 1st sess., April 18, 2007, http://rules.senate.gov/hearings/2007/ 041807correctedTranscript.pdf (accessed October 15, 2008).

8. Mann, Senate Committee, *Repealing the Limitation on Party Expenditures on Behalf of Candidates in General Elections* [S 1091], 110th Cong., 1st sess., April 18, 2007, available at http://rules.senate.gov/hearings/2007/041807Mann.pdf (accessed September 18, 2008).

9. Ibid.

10. *FEC v. Wisconsin Right to Life, Inc.*, 127 S. Ct. 2652, 2672 (2007).

11. Michael Malbin, testimony, Senate Committee on Rules and Administration, *Repealing the Limitation on Party Expenditures on Behalf of Candidates in General Elections* [S 1091], 110th Cong., 1st sess., April 18, 2007, http://rules.senate.gov/hearings/2007/041807Malbin.pdf (accessed October 15, 2008).

Index

About the Authors

Peter J. Wallison is a senior fellow at the American Enterprise Institute, where he also co-directs AEI's Project on Financial Market Deregulation and holds the Arthur F. Burns Chair in Financial Policy Studies. He served as general counsel of the United States Treasury Department (1981–85), and subsequently as White House counsel to President Ronald Reagan (1986–87). Between 1972 and 1976, he served first as special assistant to New York Governor Nelson A. Rockefeller and, subsequently, as counsel to Mr. Rockefeller when he was vice president of the United States. Mr. Wallison is the author of *Ronald Reagan: The Power of Conviction and the Success of His Presidency* (Westview Press, 2002). He is also the author of *Back from the Brink* (AEI Press, 1990), a proposal for a private deposit insurance system, and co-author of *Nationalizing Mortgage Risk: The Growth of Fannie Mae and Freddie Mac* (AEI Press, 2000), *The GAAP Gap: Corporate Disclosure in the Internet Age* (AEI Press, 2000), and *Competitive Equity: A Better Way to Organize Mutual Funds* (AEI Press, 2007). He is also the editor of *Optional Federal Chartering and Regulation of Insurance Companies* (AEI Press, 2000), *Serving Two Masters, Yet Out of Control: Fannie Mae and Freddie Mac* (AEI Press, 2001).

Joel M. Gora has been a professor of law at Brooklyn Law School for thirty years, teaching courses in constitutional law, election law and civil procedure, and serving two separate terms as the law school's Associate Dean for Academic Affairs. Mr. Gora has also been a long-time lawyer for the American Civil Liberties Union. During his ACLU career, he has worked on a number of landmark Supreme Court cases, including all of the Court's significant campaign finance decisions, starting with Buckley v. Valeo in 1976, which he personally argued before the High Court. Professor Gora is the author of several books dealing with constitutional law themes, including *The Rights* *of Reporters* (Avon Books, 1974), *Due Process of Law* (National Textbook Company, 1977), *The Right to Protest* (Southern Illinois University Press, 1991, co-authored), and a number of articles about the constitutional problems posed by campaign finance regulation and other First Amendment matters.